curry lover's
cookbook

mridula baljekar
curry lover's
cookbook

deliciously spicy and aromatic Indian dishes

southwater

This edition is published by Southwater, an imprint of Anness Publishing Ltd,
108 Great Russell Street, London WC1B 3NA; info@anness.com

www.southwaterbooks.com; www.annesspublishing.com; twitter: @Anness_Books

If you like the images in this book and would like to investigate using them for publishing, promotions
or advertising, please visit our website www.practicalpictures.com for more information.

© Anness Publishing Ltd 2016

Publisher: Joanna Lorenz
Project Editor: Sarah Ainley
Designer: Nigel Partridge
Jacket Design: Balley Design
Reference section: Mridula Baljekar
Recipes: Mridula Baljekar, Rafi Fernandez, Shehzad Husain,
Christine Ingram, Manisha Kanani, Sally Mansfield, and Jennie Shapter
Photography: Edward Allwright, David Armstrong, Nicki Dowey, Amanda Heywood,
Ferguson Hill, Janine Hosegood, David Jordan, David King, Patrick McLeavey and Sam Stowell
Map Illustrations: David Cook at Linden Artists Limited
Production Controller: Pirong Wang

PICTURE CREDITS
Additional picture material supplied by Life File:
page 8, page 9 top, page 10, page 11 top and bottom.

PUBLISHER'S NOTE
Although the advice and information in this book are believed to be accurate and true at the
time of going to press, neither the authors nor the publisher can accept any legal
responsibility or liability for any errors or omissions that may have been made nor
for any inaccuracies nor for any loss, harm or injury that comes
about from following instructions or advice in this book.

COOK'S NOTES
Bracketed terms are intended for American readers.
For all recipes, quantities are given in both metric and imperial measures and, where appropriate, in standard
cups and spoons. Follow one set of measures, but not a mixture, because they are not interchangeable.
Standard spoon and cup measures are level. 1 tsp = 5ml, 1 tbsp = 15ml, 1 cup = 250ml/8fl oz.
Australian standard tablespoons are 20ml. Australian readers should use 3 tsp
in place of 1 tbsp for measuring small quantities.
American pints are 16fl oz/2 cups. American readers should use
20fl oz/2.5 cups in place of 1 pint when measuring liquids.
Electric oven temperatures in this book are for conventional ovens. When using a fan oven, the temperature
will probably need to be reduced by about 10–20°C/20–40°F. Since ovens vary, you should
check with your manufacturer's instruction book for guidance.
Medium (US large) eggs are used unless otherwise stated.

CONTENTS

INTRODUCTION

The subcontinent of India evokes mystery, magic and romance. Steeped in history and heritage, India has a chequered past filled with exciting discoveries of new lands, great empires built and destroyed, valuable allies and dangerous enemies. Central to the dramas that have unfolded in the region are the exotic spices that have been grown here for centuries. It is carefully prepared blends of these spices that provide the mouthwatering tastes, flavours and aromas of curries.

Below: Pork balchao, from Goa, is one of only a few Indian pork recipes, dating back to when Goa was a Portuguese colony.

India has long been known as the spice bowl of the world. The use of premium quality spices in this sun-drenched, monsoon-fed land was an established way of life long before traders, among them Moguls, Persians, English, Syrians, Portuguese, and French came to the area, all lured by the valuable spices.

Spectacular geography, fascinating ancient customs, and glorious foods all continue to draw foreigners to this magical land. From the border with Afghanistan in the north to the beaches of Goa in the west, and down to Sri Lanka in the south, this corner of the world is diverse in every respect. Just as much as the

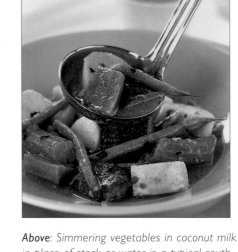

Above: Simmering vegetables in coconut milk in place of stock or water is a typical south Indian cooking technique.

beautiful scenery, culinary traditions have also been influenced by geographical and climatic conditions. With vast distances to be travelled, and no means of transporting fresh produce efficiently, cooks have made the best use of the ingredients available locally.

Besides offering fabulous flavours, Indian cooking is also extremely healthy. The emphasis is firmly on

Below: This rich fish curry, known as kalia, *originates from Bengal, in eastern India.*

freshness, with a wide range of meats, fish and shellfish, vegetables and salads, together with wheat or rice as the staple. Meat and fish are served in small quantities, surrounded by inviting little side dishes, such as pickles, chutneys and salads, flavoured with fresh herbs, chillies or yogurt, and used as seasonings. Rice or breads in India form the staple diet. What is more, many of the ingredients used in these dishes are known for their medicinal properties. For example, there is strong evidence that garlic and fresh root ginger, two of the most essential ingredients in curries, contain properties that can help to combat heart diseases and stomach ulcers respectively.

The striking resemblance in many of the cooking and serving styles throughout regional India is reflected in the ingredients used. The exquisite flavour of cardamom pods, the warmth of cumin, the sweet, mellow taste of coriander, the woody aroma of ginger and fiery chillies are characteristic flavours, adding zest and flavour to countless curries.

As well as the local dishes based on traditional culinary techniques, there are cooking styles in practice in India which have been introduced by foreign powers over the course of the country's history. The north continues to be dominated by Mogul cuisine, while the east has tribal and Anglo-Indian styles. In the south, Syrian Jews and French traders contributed techniques, and western India came under the influence of the Portuguese and the Persians. The result is a colourful cuisine of great richness and depth, with a repertoire of recipes that is virtually unmatched anywhere else in the world.

Above: *Beef biryani is a speciality dish from the Muslim community in India.*

Culinary skills and expertise from around the world have been developed in India, and the best of the resulting dishes are featured in this wonderful collection. The aim of this volume is to offer traditional regional curry recipes with authentic flavours and uncomplicated preparation and cooking methods. I hope it will encourage even novice cooks to get to know the delights of cooking hot and spicy curries.

MRIDULA BALJEKAR

Below: *Potatoes with roasted poppy seeds, a classic dish from eastern India.*

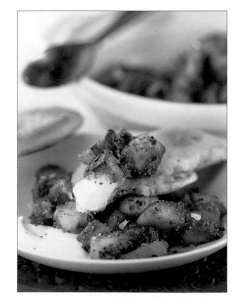

CULTURE and CUISINE

India is a vast country, with a total area of around 3.3 million square kilometres (1.3 million square miles) and a population in excess of 1 billion. It is a land of striking contrasts, with huge variations in terms of climate, geography, religion, culture and customs. All of these factors have had a powerful influence on the country's cuisine, which has emerged as one of the most rich and diverse in the world.

The country's various climates, affected by a wide range of geographical conditions, naturally dictate the types of crops that are grown in different regions. In the past, when transport and communications were poor, people had to confine themselves to the ingredients that grew naturally in their local area.

They created a vast array of recipes, with distinct variations between each region.

Religion also played an important role in the development of Indian cuisine. Many religions exist side by side in India, with Hinduism being the indigenous faith. The Sikh and Buddhist religions are both branches of Hinduism. Islam was introduced by foreign traders, and went on to become one of the main religions of the land. Both the Hindu and Muslim religions have certain taboos as far as food is concerned. Hinduism prohibits the eating of beef: the cow is regarded as sacred because Hindu mythology depicts it as the companion of one of the most important Hindu gods, Lord Krishna. The Koran, on the other hand, prohibits the consumption of pork, so

beef has become popular among people of the Muslim faith, and an excellent range of beef-based recipes is found across the country. Although pork is not generally eaten by Hindus, the Christians of Goa, on the west coast, and the warrior community in Coorg, in the South, have created a variety of delicious recipes for pork.

Cultures and customs have also had a considerable impact on Indian cuisine. Over the centuries, historical events have imposed many different cultures upon India, and the country has not only absorbed them, but has also encouraged each to flourish individually.

Below: Hessian sacks of fresh and dried chillies for sale in an Indian street.

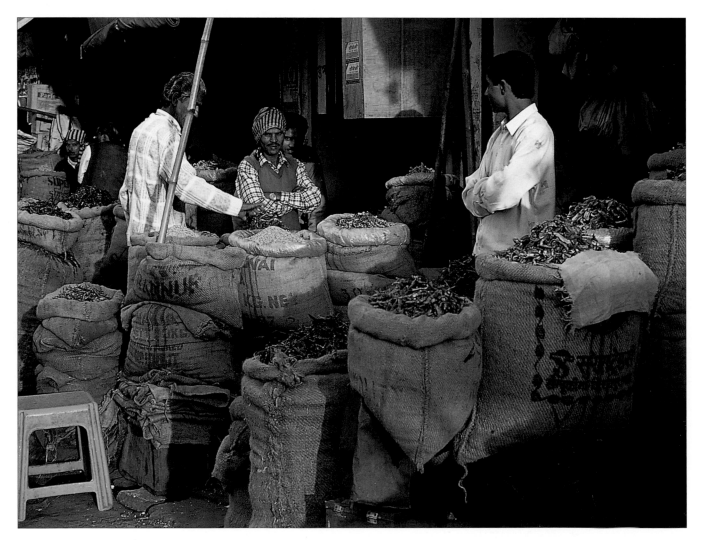

REGIONAL DIVERSITY

The diversity of the food culture across the regions of modern-day India may not be as pronounced as it once was, but in a country so vast it is inevitable that long-standing traditions for produce and cooking styles have persisted.

North India

The northern states of India have been subjected to a vast number of foreign invaders, traders and pilgrims throughout history. The north, more than any other region, allows easy access into India, with the Khyber Pass providing a natural link between Afghanistan and present-day Pakistan. Groups of travellers have entered through this long, narrow pass

Below: *The huge expanse of land that is India reaches from neighbouring Afghanistan in the far north to Sri Lanka in the south.*

Above: *Indian housewives shop daily for fresh ingredients at the vegetable market.*

and spread themselves all over the area. Most notable were the Moguls, who invaded India in the 16th century and ruled for almost three hundred years.

During their journey to India, the Moguls came across the much-admired Persian style of cooking, which they adapted and introduced to India. This has become known as Mughlai cuisine, and is now almost as widely eaten in the West as it is in India. Foreign travellers are also credited with introducing exotic fruits and nuts to Kashmir, where they were used to create a variety of sumptuous dishes. Kashmiri cuisine is prized for its unusual richness and varied textures and flavours, and dishes such as kormas, pasandas and biryanis are now firmly established as some of the most popular foods of northern India.

From Kashmir, the Moguls spread south and west into the Punjab, which is renowned for its tandoori cooking. Punjab is also known as the bread box of India, for the enormous variety of breads, both leavened and unleavened, it produces. Naan is the most widely eaten bread among the leavened variety,

Above: Rice is the staple food of southern and eastern India, and a plentiful harvest is essential for the survival of these regions.

while tandoori rotis, which is cooked in a tandoor, or Indian clay oven, is the most common unleavened bread.

Delhi, the capital of India, was once the centre of the Mogul dynasty. The Moguls' love of fine food, along with their exquisite taste in fine art and architecture, are so deeply rooted in Delhi that the city is now a major tourist attraction. As well as the traditional Mughlai food, Punjabi food, which includes a wonderful range of sweets (candies), has made Delhi a true food lover's paradise.

East India

The influence of Mogul cuisine is not so pronounced in the eastern region, where local styles of cooking have more of a stronghold. The state of Bengal, for example, has developed in almost total isolation despite its proximity to the northern states. Apart from some minor reminders of the Moguls' brief presence in the region, Bengal has a unique cuisine, which is famous all over India.

Bengalis have always been very proud of their produce, and have made full use of home-grown ingredients to create a fascinating style of cooking. Mustard grows extensively in the area and mustard oil is widely used as a cooking medium. Several vegetarian, meat and poultry dishes also make use of ground mustard. Coconut, another local product, is widely used in both sweet and savoury dishes. Bengalis are immensely proud of the rice grown in their soil, and of the fish found in the waters of the Bay of Bengal. Together, rice and fish curry constitute the everyday diet of the Bengali people, although the state's most significant contribution to Indian cuisine is generally regarded to be its superb range of sweets.

Kolkata (formerly Calcutta), the capital of West Bengal, has a strong tradition for Anglo-Indian cuisine, which is popular among the city's Anglo-Indian community, and in the clubs and sports centres established by the British Raj in the 19th century. These eccentrically outmoded institutions still thrive in the old British manner: cocktails are served by liveried staff, and are accompanied by delicious tidbits, cooked in the Western style but flavoured with Indian spices.

The streets of Kolkata are bustling with vendors selling all kinds of tempting local and Anglo-Indian sweet and savoury snacks. Ghugni, a spiced chickpea dish served with mouthwatering relishes, is one of the favourite local dishes.

Although the food of Bihar and Orissa, two other eastern states, has not made any significant impact on the cuisine of the subcontinent, Orissa deserves a mention for its excellent fresh fish and shellfish, which it exports worldwide in large quantities.

South India

The southern states have been greatly influenced by the indigenous Hindu faith. On the southern tip of the country, however, the Malabar Coast provided easy access to the French, Dutch, British and Portuguese, as well as to a small number of Jews from Syria. The French had some influence on the cuisine of this area in the state of Pondicherry, and the Jews contributed meat and poultry dishes to Kerala. As well as making their mark on the eastern region, the British had thriving trading posts in Chennai (formerly Madras), and an Anglo-Indian community still exists in that area. Otherwise, since the Dutch had no impact on Indian cuisine, and the Portuguese were concentrated in Goa, southern India has remained free of foreign influence seen elsewhere.

South Indian food is quite different from the rich cuisine of the north. It is light and refreshing, and the sauces are enriched with coconut milk, whereas in northern India, dairy cream and nuts are used for the same purpose. The food in the south is generally fiery: the temperature here is hot throughout the year, and chillies are known to have a cooling effect on the body.

Along the coast of southern India, fish curry and rice are eaten on an almost daily basis, but there are two dishes for which South India is famous. Dosas, paper-thin pancakes made from ground rice and lentils, are filled with spicy vegetables and served for breakfast with a coconut chutney, while idlis, which are steamed rice dumplings, are eaten with spicy lentils and chutneys.

Between Maharashtra in the west and the Bay of Bengal in the east, lies the state of Andhra Pradesh, which is

Above: *Numerous varieties of beans, peas and lentils are on sale in this pulse shop, along with spice mixes for cooking them.*

famous for its forts and palaces, and for its unique cuisine. Mogul traditions are strong here: even though the state has never been ruled by the Muslim rulers, the last Mogul emperor retired to the capital city Hyderabad, causing a culinary revolution that influenced the whole region. Kababs, biryanis and kormas exist side by side with hot, fiery local foods and a wide variety of rice, which is grown locally.

West India

In western India lies the state of Gujarat. Most Gujaratis are strictly vegetarian and, unlike the many non-meat eaters in India who eat fish, they eat neither fish nor eggs. Their religion emphasizes the respect that must be shown to all living beings, and prohibits the taking of any life for reasons of personal enjoyment. As a result, the Gujaratis have truly perfected the art of vegetarian cooking. Fresh vegetables, lentils, beans, peas and dairy products have taken centre stage, and dairy products are abundant. People take yogurt and buttermilk on a daily basis, and use them in cooking. Breads

are skilfully made, using both millet flour and maize flour (cornmeal).

The most famous culinary export of Gujarat is the vegetable- and lentil-based dhansak. About 13 centuries ago, a group of Persians fled their country to avoid religious persecution. Gujarat, being open to the sea, was the most convenient point from which to enter India. The Persians were made to feel

at home here, and became known as the Parsis. They adapted the rich and varied culture of Gujarat and eventually spread further west, to Mumbai.

Mumbai (formerly Bombay) is situated on the edge of the deep blue Arabian Sea, and it is here that the Gateway of India was built during the British Raj, to commemorate a visit by the Prince of Wales. Mumbai is the capital of Maharashtra, a mainly vegetarian state with a cosmopolitan population that has given rise to a rich and varied cuisine. Mumbai is probably the only city in India where food from almost any part of the country can be sampled. As well as Indian food, Chinese dishes with an Indian twist can be found in the numerous restaurants throughout this vibrant city. Fresh fish and shellfish are also plentiful in the area.

To the south of Mumbai is Goa, where the lure of Indian spices brought Portuguese traders, who colonized the area. Goa remained under Portuguese rule until 1962, and the influence the Portuguese left behind has created a happy marriage between East and West. Goa's most famous export is vindaloo, which has Portuguese origins.

Below: *Fisherman inspect their early morning catch on the beaches of Kerala.*

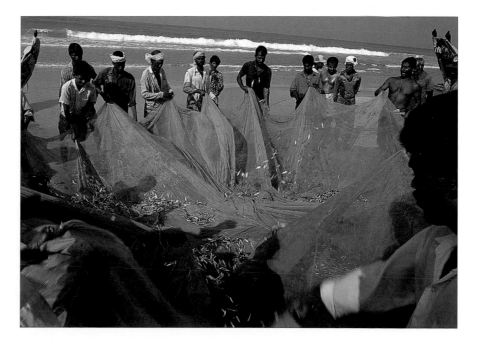

PRINCIPLES of INDIAN COOKING

Until recently, no written record of Indian recipes has existed in India itself. Recipes have traditionally been handed down from one generation to another. Far from being a disadvantage, this has actually helped to fire the imagination of the creative cook, and many dishes that first started out as experiments in spice blends and flavour combinations have now become world classics.

Spices and aromatics

The key to successful Indian cooking lies in the art of blending spices and herbs, rather than sophisticated cooking techniques. The traditional Indian cook relies on instinct rather than written recipes when measuring and combining spices, and in this way unique and very personal tastes can be created. This is one reason why the same dish from one region can look and taste quite different, according to who has cooked it.

Herbs are added to a dish during the cooking time to add flavour and aroma, but spices, including those used mainly for taste or for aroma, perform a more complex role.

Spices can be divided into two main groups: those that are integrated into a dish by the end of the cooking process, and those that are removed. The spices in the first group add taste, texture and colour. Different combinations are used, and no single spice is allowed to dominate the final flavour. Useful spices in this group include coriander, cumin, turmeric and garam masala, all in ground form.

The second group of spices add aroma to a dish. They remain identifiable at the end of cooking, as most of them are used whole. Once these spices have released their aroma, their function is complete and they are not eaten, but removed from the dish before serving or simply left on one side of the plate. Examples of this type of spice are whole cloves, cardamom pods, cinnamon sticks and bay leaves. These spices can also be ground, in which case they will blend into the sauce during cooking, and will be eaten in the dish in the same way as any other ground spice.

Adding flavour

Having chosen which spices to use, you can then decide what kind of flavours you would like to create. For instance, dry-roasting and grinding flavouring ingredients before adding them to a dish creates a completely different taste and aroma from frying the raw ground spices in hot fat before adding the main ingredients. The flavour of a dish will also vary according to the sequence in which the spices are added, and the length of time each spice is fried and allowed to release its flavour.

Indian cooking lends itself to being personalized by different cooks, and with even just two or three spices, you can create distinctly varied dishes.

Below: Spices and seasonings are what gives Indian food its unique character.

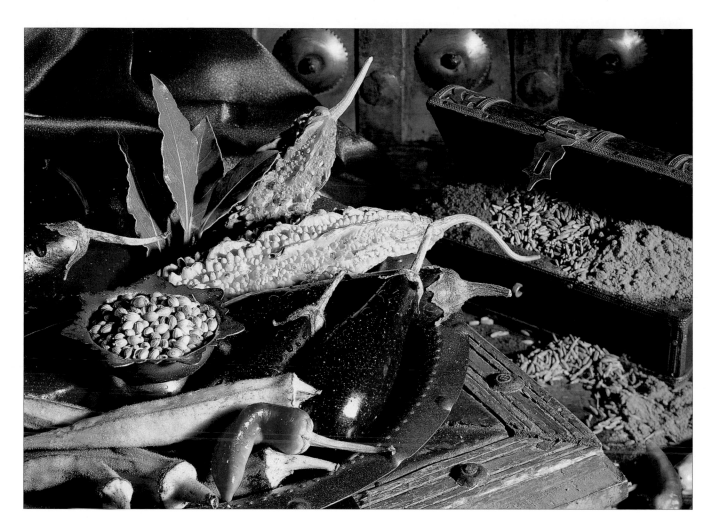

What is a curry?

In India, the word curry refers to a sauce or gravy used as an accompaniment to moisten grains of *chawal* (rice) or to make *rotis* (bread) more enjoyable. The rice or bread are considered the main dish of the meal.

The word curry is generally believed to be an anglicized version of the south Indian word *kaari*. It belongs to the Tamil language, which is spoken in the state of Tamil Nadu, of which Madras is the capital. In Tamil, the word means sauce and it is thought that when the British were active in this area, the spelling was somehow changed to curry. Other theories suggest that the word *cury* has existed in English in the context of cooking since the 14th century, and that it was originally derived from the French verb *cuire* (to cook).

The main ingredients of a curry can vary enormously, and two highly dissimilar dishes can be equally deserving of the name. Even the lentil dish known as *dhal*, which bears no resemblance to a sauce, falls under the definition of a curry; in India, *dhal-chawal* and *dhal-roti* are eaten on a daily basis.

A vegetable curry usually consists of a selection of fresh vegetables cooked in a sauce, which can have a thick or a thin consistency, depending on the style of cooking in the region. The sauces for meat, poultry and fish curries also vary in consistency, and are all designed to be served with rice or bread. Gujarat in the west and Punjab in the north also make spiced curries using just yogurt mixed with a little *besan* (gram flour). Made without meat, poultry or vegetables, these dishes are known as *khadis*.

Above: Most of the key ingredients needed for Indian curries are now available from large supermarkets, but Indian food stores will usually stock a wider selection.

What to eat with a curry

In south and eastern India, curries are always served with rice, which, as the region's main crop, is the staple food of the area, and is eaten daily. Wheat grows abundantly in north India, and in most northern regions, breads such as naan, chapatis and parathas are eaten with curries and with dry, spiced vegetable and lentil dishes. In the Punjab region, however, breads made from *besan* and *makki* (cornmeal) are more usually served with curries. In western India, curries are eaten with breads made with flour prepared from *jowar* (millet) and *bajra* (milo).

PREPARING an INDIAN CURRY

While there may be no such thing as a definitive curry recipe, there certainly is an established procedure to follow when preparing a curry. Deciding what type of curry you are going to make is the first step. Choose your main ingredient, and select your cooking pan accordingly, as this will affect the ultimate success of the dish. A deep-sided pan will be necessary if the curry is to contain lots of liquid, while for fish, a wide, flat pan is needed to allow the pieces of fish to be laid flat, side by side, in a single layer.

Cooking fats
You need to decide whether you want to use ghee, which is clarified butter, or oil as your cooking medium. Traditionally, the Indian housewife would use ghee, not just for its rich flavour, but also because dairy products are believed to be more nutritious. Modern Indian families are now deviating from this practice, however, because of a growing awareness of the dangers of eating too much saturated fat. Sunflower, vegetable and corn oils will all make suitable alternatives. Olive oil is not normally used, although a basic cooking version (not virgin or extra virgin) will work perfectly well. Ghee can be reserved for special occasion dishes, if you like.

Cooking liquids
Most curries are water-based. Stock is sometimes used in Indian cooking, but it is not a common practice as meat is always cooked on the bone, and this creates a sufficiently robust flavour. Whether you use stock or water as your cooking liquid, it is important to make sure the liquid is at least lukewarm. Adding cold liquid to carefully blended spices will impair the flavours.

Adding salt
Pay careful attention when using salt in an Indian dish. Do not be afraid to use the amount specified in a recipe; even if it seems a lot, it will have been worked out to achieve an overall balance of flavours. There are now several brands of low-sodium salt on the market, which can be substituted, if you prefer.

Above: Fresh and dried herbs provide colour, flavour, aroma and texture to Indian food.

Thickening agents
Indian cooking does not rely on flour to thicken sauces. Instead, the consistency is more usually achieved by adding ingredients such as dairy cream or coconut cream, nut pastes, onion purée, tomatoes, and ground seeds such as poppy, sesame and sunflower.

Adding colour
Some of the ingredients added to curries not only determine their texture and consistency, but also their colour. In Mughlai sauces and curries, the onions are softened but not browned, which gives the dishes their distinctive pale colour. Bhuna (stir-fried) curries, on the other hand, brown the onions, making the final dishes reddish-brown in colour.

Souring agents
Some of the souring agents used in curries also affect their colour and consistency. Tamarind, for instance, darkens and thickens a sauce at the same time. Lime, lemon and white vinegar, however, will neither alter the colour of a curry nor thicken it, and a thickening agent such as coconut milk or a nut or seed paste has to be used as well. Ingredients such as dry mango powder (*amchur*), dried pomegranate

COLOURING INGREDIENTS
The depth of the curry's colour will depend on the amount of colorant used in relation to other ingredients.
turmeric: bright yellow
saffron: pale apricot
red chillies: reddish brown
fresh coriander (cilantro) leaves: green
tomatoes: reddish, if used alone; pinkish if combined with yogurt
onions: brown
ground coriander: deep brown if fried for 5–6 minutes
garam masala: deep brown if fried for 1 minute

seeds (known as *anardana*), as well as tomatoes and yogurts are all used to lend a distinctive tangy flavour to a curry, and they will also affect the colour to varying degrees.

Adding heat

The most important ingredient for achieving a fiery flavour and appearance is chilli. Although chillies were unknown in India before the Portuguese settlers introduced them in the 15th century, it is difficult to imagine Indian food without them today. It is chilli in its powdered form that contributes to the colour of a curry, and chilli powder is readily available in a range of heat levels. Always be sure to check the label carefully. If you want the curry to be appealing to the eye without scorching the taste buds, choose a chilli powder made from either Kashmiri or Byadigi chillies. This will lend a rich colour to the dish, but the flavour will be fairly mild. You can always use it in conjunction with a hot chilli powder if you prefer to give the curry some kick. Another way to achieve both colour and heat in the same dish is to combine chilli powder with fresh chillies: fresh chillies are always hotter than dried.

When buying fresh chillies, try to find the ones used in Indian cooking, rather than Mexican varieties. Those used in Indian cooking are long and slim, and are sometimes labelled "finger chillies". Thai chillies make a good substitute, and are available from Asian food stores.

Paste made from dried red chillies also gives a very good colour and quite a different flavour from chilli powder. To make it, all you need to do is to soak the chillies for 15–20 minutes in hot water and then purée them. The paste will keep well in an airtight jar in the refrigerator for 4–5 days.

Cooking a curry

Several factors will influence the making of a good curry, and one of the most important of these is the cooking temperature. The fat should be heated to the right temperature and maintained at a steady heat until the spices have released their flavour. A heavy pan, such as a wok, karahi or large pan, will help to maintain the temperature, so that the spices can cook without burning. While recipes may vary, the usual procedure is to start off by cooking the onions over a medium heat. Once the onions have softened, the ground spices are added and the temperature is lowered.

Another important factor is the chopping of the onions. The finer the onion is chopped, the better it will blend into the sauce. In many recipes, onion, ginger and garlic are puréed to make a

Below: The secret of Indian cooking lies in the use of spices, and blending spices at home will give more flavoursome curries.

wet spice paste, which is fried until all the moisture has evaporated, before the ground spices are added. It is crucial to follow the timings specified in a recipe for each of these cooking stages.

Adding spices in the correct sequence is also vital. While some spices take only a few seconds to release their flavour, others need a few minutes, and if you add spices that require less cooking time together with those that need more, some will burn and others will remain raw. The simplest way to avoid this is to keep to the order in which the spices are listed in the recipe, and to be very exact about following the specified cooking time for each ingredient.

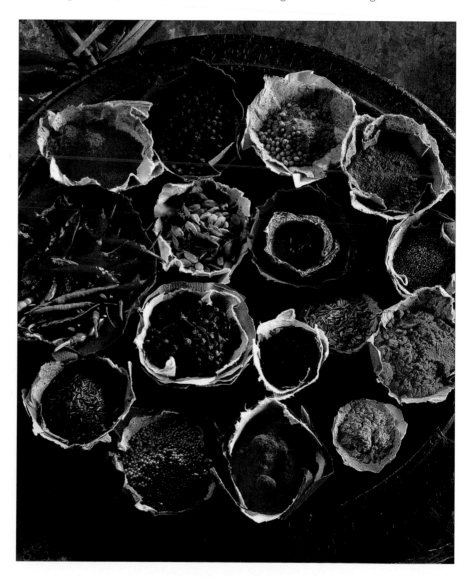

PLANNING an INDIAN MEAL

When planning your menu, always bear in mind that an everyday Indian meal features only three items: the main dish, a side dish and a staple, which would be rice or bread. Chutneys, salads and raitas can also be served to add a tangy taste.

Planning the menu

When deciding which foods to serve, consider the main dish. Is it going to be highly spiced, such as a vindaloo or a bhuna? Or will it have subtle flavours, such as a korma or a pasanda? A little careful planning will ensure that the flavours of the dishes complement, rather than compete with, each other. Choose the side dish according to the strength of the main one. A lightly spiced

Below: There is no rigid structure to an Indian meal, but there should always be a good balance of dry and moist dishes.

side dish is more enjoyable when the main dish is spicier. This does not apply in reverse, however, and a side dish with complex spicing is not the ideal accompaniment to a mild main dish.

Dishes with a drier consistency are generally accompanied by a vegetable curry or a lentil dish. Biryanis and pilaus are traditionally served with a simple raita, although they are more usually served with a vegetable curry in Indian restaurants in the West.

How to serve

An Indian meal is not served as separate courses, with an appetizer, followed by a main dish and one or two side dishes. Although the meal will usually consist of several dishes, all complement each other and are brought to the table at the same time, with diners helping themselves to each dish in any order.

> **USEFUL STANDBYS**
> • Use bottled ginger and garlic purées (paste) rather than peeling and chopping the fresh spices.
> • Canned chopped tomatoes can be used instead of fresh tomatoes, although you may need to increase the quantities of souring agent, salt and chilli to compensate for the depleted flavour.
> • Canned or packet creamed coconut is a convenient replacement for fresh coconut. Use according to the manufacturer's instructions.

For entertaining and more lavish occasions, you can add other dishes to the standard three-dish Indian menu. One or two dry meat dishes, such as a kabab or tandoori chicken, in addition to some chutneys, pickles, raitas and poppadums, with a dessert to follow, can turn an ordinary family meal into dinner-party fare.

Indian desserts

In India, a meal will usually end with fresh fruit, rather than elaborate or cooked desserts. Fruits can be served with real flair, however, and are often combined with other ingredients to create imaginative and exciting flavours. Choose one or two exotic fruits, such as papaya, pomegranate or star fruit, and combine them with everyday fruits in a fruit salad. Serve with Greek (US strained plain) yogurt flavoured with rose water and a little ground cardamom.

Indian sweets (candies) are quite heavy and are served as a snack with tea and coffee, in the same way as cakes and biscuits (cookies) are eaten in the West.

COOKING FOR A PARTY

It is a good idea to cook the curry dishes a day ahead of the party, storing them in the refrigerator until you are ready to reheat them. Accompanying dhal dishes can also be prepared 24 hours in advance, although the seasonings should not be added until just before serving. You can prepare vegetables in advance, but do not cook them more than a few hours ahead. Likewise, you can prepare ingredients for raitas a day ahead, but do not assemble them until a few hours before they are needed; the yogurt for raitas should always be fresh. Pickles and chutneys will benefit from advance preparation, but follow individual recipes for timing guides, as some will deteriorate more quickly than others. The bread dough for rotis can be made the day before. The rotis can be made 2 hours before you plan to serve them. Spread them with butter and wrap in foil to keep warm, then set them aside; reheat in the oven before serving.

Freezing curries

In today's busy world, it is not always possible to serve a meal while it is still sizzling in the pan. If you are entertaining, you may prefer to cook the curry in advance to save yourself time on the day, or you may like to cook a larger quantity than you will need and freeze some for another meal; you may even have leftovers.

Spicy food is ideal for freezing as the flavours seem to improve when the food is thawed and reheated. Most of the spices used in Indian cooking have natural preservative qualities, as does the acid in souring agents. However, you should bear in mind the following factors if cooking specifically for the freezer:
• Leave the food slightly underdone.
• Cool the food rapidly. The best way to do this is to tip it into a large tray (a large roasting pan is ideal) and leave it in a cool place.
• Once the food has cooled completely, spoon it into plastic containers, then label and chill it in the refrigerator for a couple of hours, before transferring it to the freezer. The food will keep in the freezer for 6–8 months, depending on the star rating of your freezer.

Food that you did not plan to freeze, such as leftovers, should not be kept in the freezer for longer than 2–3 months, again, depending on the efficiency of your freezer. Meat and poultry curries freeze very successfully, as do curries made from vegetables, lentils and pulses. Fish curries can be frozen, but they are generally less successful as changes in the water balance may damage the more delicate texture of cooked fish.

Thawing and reheating

It is important to thaw frozen food thoroughly and slowly. Leave it in the refrigerator for 18–24 hours before reheating. After reheating, always make sure the food is piping hot before serving. These steps are crucial in order to ensure that any potentially harmful bacteria are destroyed. If you have a temperature probe, check that the reheated food is at least 85°C/185°F right the way through before serving.

REHEATING LEFTOVERS

This method will make leftover food that has been frozen taste really fresh. The method can also be used to reheat food that has been stored for a day or two in the refrigerator.

Heat about 10ml/2 tsp vegetable oil in a wok, karahi or large pan over a medium heat. Add up to 1.5ml/¼ tsp garam masala (depending on the quantity of food), and allow to bubble gently for 10–15 seconds. Add the thawed food to the pan and increase the heat to high. Let the food bubble or sizzle in the pan until it is heated through, stirring from time to time to make sure the heat is well distributed. Add a little water if the food looks particularly dry. Stir in 15ml/1 tbsp chopped fresh coriander (cilantro). Remove from the heat, transfer to a warmed platter and serve immediately.

A certain amount of water separation is to be expected as a defrosted dish thaws out. The dish will return to its normal consistency when it is reheated, as the water will be reabsorbed by the meat or vegetables.

Thawed food can be reheated in the microwave or in a covered casserole on the stove top. If using a microwave, cover the food with microwave cling film (plastic wrap). Stir the food from time to time as it is heated, to ensure the heat passes right the way through. You may need to add a small amount of water when reheating, to ensure that the dish does not dry out.

AROMATICS, SPICES and HERBS

Spices are integral to both the flavour and aroma of a dish. Some spices are used principally for the taste they impart, while other spices, known as aromatics, are used mainly for their aroma. One individual spice can completely alter the taste of a dish and a combination of several spices will also affect its colour and texture.

The quantities of spices and salt specified in recipes are measured to achieve a balance of flavours, although you may prefer to increase or decrease the quantities according to taste. This is particularly true of fresh chillies and chilli powder: experiment with quantities, adding less or more than specified.

Fresh and dried herbs also play an important part in the combinations of colour, flavour, aroma and texture that make up a curry. Because herbs require only a minimal amount of cooking, they retain a marvellous intensity of flavour and fragrance.

Garlic
Widely available fresh and dried, garlic is used for its strong, aromatic flavour, and is a standard ingredient, along with ginger, in most curries. Fresh garlic can be pulped, crushed or chopped, or the cloves can be used whole. Garlic powder is mainly used in spice mixtures.

Ginger
One of the most popular spices in India and also one of the oldest, fresh root ginger is an important ingredient in many Indian curries. Its refreshing scent is reminiscent of citrus and it has a pleasant, sharp flavour. The root should be plump with a fairly smooth skin, which is peeled off before use. Young root ginger is tender and mild, whereas older roots are quite fibrous, with a more pungent flavour. Dried powdered ginger is a useful standby, but the flavour is not quite the same. It is often blended with other spices to make curry powder.

PULPING GARLIC
Fresh garlic is used so often in Indian cooking that you may find it more practical to prepare garlic in bulk and store in the refrigerator or freezer until needed.

Separate the garlic bulb into cloves and peel off the papery skin. Process the whole cloves in a food processor until smooth. Freeze the garlic pulp in ice-cube trays used specially for the purpose. Put 5ml/ 1 tsp in each compartment, freeze, remove from the tray and store in the freezer in a sealed plastic bag. Alternatively, store the pulp in an airtight container in the refrigerator for 3–4 weeks.

Below: Fresh root ginger

Below: Ground ginger

PREPARING FRESH ROOT GINGER
Fresh root ginger has a delightfully clean and pungent taste, and is easy to prepare. It is widely available from supermarkets and markets.

To grate ginger, carefully remove the skin using a sharp knife or vegetable peeler. Grate the peeled ginger using the fine side of a metal cheese grater. To chop, slice the ginger into fine strips, then chop as required.

PULPING FRESH ROOT GINGER
Pulped fresh root ginger is time-consuming to prepare for each individual recipe. Instead, prepare a large quantity and store in the freezer until needed.

Peel off the tough outer skin using a sharp knife or a vegetable peeler. Roughly chop, then process in a food processor, adding a little water to get a smooth consistency. Store the pulp in the refrigerator for 3–4 weeks or freeze in ice-cube trays used for the purpose.

Left: Green and red Bird's eye chillies

Chillies

These hot peppers belong to the genus capsicum, along with sweet (bell) peppers. Some varieties are extremely fiery and all chillies should be used with caution. Much of the severe heat of fresh chillies is contained in the seeds, and the heat can be toned down by removing these before use. Like other spicy foods, chillies are perfect for hot climates as

they cause blood to rush to the surface of the skin, promoting instant cooling.

Chillies vary in size and colour, but as a rule, dark green chillies tend to be hotter than light green ones. Red chillies are usually hotter still, and some will darken to brown or black when fully ripe. Shape and colour give no sure indication of the hotness, and it is wise to be wary of any unfamiliar variety. Dried chillies can be used whole or coarsely crushed.

Chilli powder is a fiery ground spice that should be used with great caution. The heat varies from brand to brand, so adjust quantities to suit your taste buds. Some brands include other spices and herbs, as well as ground chillies, and these may not be appropriate to the dish you are cooking. Always check the label carefully.

PREPARING DRIED CHILLIES

Dried chillies are available from good supermarkets and Indian food stores.

To prepare the chillies, remove the stems and seeds, then break each chilli into two or three pieces. Put the pieces in a small bowl and cover with hot water. Leave to stand for 30 minutes, then drain (using the soaking water in the recipe, if appropriate). Use the chilli pieces as they are, or chop them finely.

WATCHPOINT

All chillies contain capsaicin, an oily substance, that can cause intense irritation to sensitive skin. If you get capsaicin on your hands and transfer it to your eyes by rubbing, you will experience considerable pain. Wash hands with soapy water after handling. Dry your hands and rub a little oil into the skin to remove any stinging juices. Many cooks prefer to wear rubber (latex) gloves.

Above: The colour of chillies gives no sure indication of hotness, although red chillies are usually hotter.

PREPARING FRESH CHILLIES

Using two or more fresh chillies will make a dish quite hot. If you prefer a milder flavour, reduce the amount of chilli used, and remove the seeds and pithy membrane. If you have sensitive skin, you may prefer to wear rubber (latex) gloves to protect your hands when preparing chillies.

1 Cut the chillies in half lengthways. Remove the membranes and seeds.

2 Cut the chilli flesh lengthways into long, thin strips.

3 If required, cut the strips of chilli crossways into tiny dice.

Below: *From left, cloves, ground cinnamon, and cinnamon sticks*

Aniseed

These liquorice-flavoured seeds are used in many fried and deep-fried Indian dishes as an aid to digestion.

Cinnamon

One of the earliest known spices, cinnamon has a highly aromatic, sweet, warm flavour. It is sold ready-ground and as sticks, which are quill-like shapes rolled from the bark of the cinnamon tree. Use cinnamon sticks whole or broken, as directed in individual recipes, and remove them from the food before serving. Ground cinnamon is a useful pantry staple.

Cloves

Originally found in the Spice Islands of Indonesia, cloves were taken to the Seychelles and Mauritius early in the 18th century. Cloves are the unopened flower buds of a tree that belongs to the myrtle family. They have an aromatic and sometimes fiery flavour and an intense fragrance, and are used to flavour many sweet and savoury dishes. Cloves are usually added whole to recipes. Their warm flavour complements all rich meats, and they need no preparation. Ground cloves are one of the ingredients added to spice mixtures.

Above: *From left, cumin seeds, fenugreek and ground cumin*

Cumin

White cumin seeds are oval, ridged and greenish brown in colour. They have a strong aroma and flavour and can be used whole or ground. Ready-ground cumin powder is widely available, but it should be bought in small quantities as it loses its flavour rapidly. Black cumin seeds are dark and aromatic. They are one of the ingredients used to make garam masala, and can be used to flavour curries and rice.

Left: *Ground and fresh turmeric*

Turmeric

A member of the ginger family but without ginger's characteristic heat, turmeric is a rhizome that is indigenous to Asia. Turmeric is sometimes referred to as Indian saffron, as it shares saffron's ability to colour food yellow, although it lacks that spice's subtlety. Fresh turmeric adds a warm and slightly musky flavour to food, but it has a strong, bitter flavour and should be used sparingly. Turmeric has a natural affinity with fish, and is also used in rice, dhal and vegetable dishes.

Dhana jeera powder

This spice mixture is made from ground roasted coriander and cumin seeds. The proportions are generally two parts coriander to one part cumin.

Fennel seeds

Similar in appearance to cumin, fennel seeds have a sweet taste and are used to flavour curries. They can be chewed as a mouth-freshener after a spicy meal.

Mustard seeds

Whole black and brown mustard seeds are indigenous to India and appear often in Indian cooking. The seeds have no aroma in their raw state, but when roasted or fried in ghee or hot oil they release a rich, nutty flavour and aroma. Mustard seeds are commonly used with vegetables and dhal dishes.

Nigella seeds

This aromatic spice has a sharp and tingling taste, and is frequently used in Indian vegetarian dishes.

Onion seeds

Black, triangular shaped and aromatic, onion seeds are used in pickles and to flavour vegetable curries and lentil dishes.

Garam masala

This is a mixture of spices that can be made at home from freshly ground spices, or purchased ready-made. There is no set recipe, but a typical mixture might include black cumin seeds, peppercorns, cloves, cinnamon and black cardamom pods. Many variations on garam masala are sold commercially, as pastes ready-made in jars. These can be substituted for garam masala, and will make useful pantry standbys.

Below: *From left, paprika, whole nutmeg and grated nutmeg*

Left: *Small green cardamom pods and the larger brown variety*

Asafoetida

This seasoning is a resin with an acrid and very bitter taste and a strong odour. It is used primarily as an anti-flatulent, and only minute quantities are used in recipes. Store in a glass jar with a strong airtight seal to prevent the smell dispersing into other ingredients in the pantry.

Cardamom pods

This spice is native to India, where it is considered the most prized spice after saffron. The pods can be used whole or the husks can be removed to release the seeds; whole pods should be always removed from the dish before serving. They have a slightly pungent, but very aromatic taste. They come in three varieties: green, white and black or brown. The green and white pods can be used for both sweet and savoury dishes or to flavour rice. Black or brown pods are used only for savoury dishes.

Nutmeg

Whole nutmeg should be grated to release its sweet, nutty flavour. Grated nutmeg imparts a similar, though less intense, flavour, and makes a very useful pantry standby.

DRY-FRYING MUSTARD SEEDS

Mustard seeds release their aroma when heated so should be dry-fried before they are added to a dish.

Heat a little ghee or vegetable oil in a wok, karahi or large pan, and add the mustard seeds. Shake the pan over the heat until the seeds start to change colour. Stir the seeds from time to time. Use the pan lid to stop the seeds jumping out of the pan when they start to splutter and pop.

Peppercorns

Black peppercorns are native to India, and are an essential ingredient in garam masala. White peppercorns are less aromatic, and the pink variety is mildly toxic and should only be used in small amounts. Peppercorns can be used whole or ground.

Paprika

A mild, sweet red powder, paprika is often used in place of or alongside chillies in westernized Indian cooking to add colour to a dish.

Saffron

The dried stigmas of the saffron crocus, which is native to Asia Minor, is the world's most expensive spice. To produce 450g/1lb of saffron requires 60,000 stigmas. Fortunately, only a small quantity of saffron is needed to flavour and colour a dish. Saffron is sold as threads and as a powder. It has a beautiful flavour and aroma.

Above: *From left, white, black and pink peppercorns*

Below: *From left, saffron powder and threads*

Curry leaves

Bright green and shiny, curry leaves are similar in appearance to bay leaves, but they have a different flavour. The leaves of a hardwood tree that is indigenous to India, they are widely used in Indian cooking, particularly in southern and western India (although not in Goa) and in Sri Lanka. Curry leaves have a warm fragrance with a subtle hint of sweet, green pepper or tangerine. They release their full flavour when bruised, and impart a highly distinctive flavour to curries. Curry leaves are sold dried and occasionally fresh in Indian food stores. Fresh leaves freeze well, but the dried leaves make a poor substitute, as they rapidly lose their fragrance.

Bay leaves

Indian bay leaves come from the cassia tree, which is similar to the tree from which cinnamon is taken. Bay leaves sold in the West are taken from the laurel tree. When used fresh, bay leaves have a deliciously sweet flavour, but they keep well in dried form, if stored in a cool, dark place in an airtight jar. Bay leaves are used in meat and rice dishes.

Left: *Dried curry leaves*

Below: *Bay leaves*

Below: *Fresh coriander*

Freezing fresh coriander

Fresh coriander (cilantro) is widely used in Indian cooking. Its flavour and aroma make it an important ingredient, and the fresh leaves make a attractive garnish. Buy bunches of coriander and freeze what is not required immediately.

1 Cut off the roots and any thick stalks, retaining the fine stalks.

2 Wash the leaves in cold water and leave in a strainer to drain.

3 When the leaves are dry, chop them finely and store them in small quantities in plastic bags or airtight containers in the freezer.

Coriander

There is no substitute for fresh coriander (cilantro), and the more that is used in Indian cooking the better. Coriander imparts a wonderful aroma and flavour, and is used both as an ingredient in cooking, and sprinkled over dishes as a garnish. Chopped coriander can be frozen successfully; the frozen coriander does not need to be defrosted before use. Coriander seeds and ground coriander powder are used for flavouring. The seeds have a pungent, slightly lemony flavour, and are used coarsely ground in meat, fish and poultry dishes. Ground coriander, a brownish powder, is an important constituent of any curry spice mixture.

Mint

There are many varieties of mint available, and the stronger-flavoured types tend to be used in Indian cooking. These taste slightly sweet and have a cool aftertaste. Mint has a fresh, stimulating aroma and is traditionally used with lamb, as well as for flavouring some vegetables, and for making chutneys and refreshing raitas. Mint is added at the end of cooking time, in order to retain the flavour.

Fenugreek

Fresh fenugreek is generally sold in bunches. It has very small leaves and is used to flavour meat and vegetarian dishes. Always discard the stalks, which will impart an unpleasant bitterness to a dish if used. Fenugreek seeds are flat, extremely pungent and slightly bitter. They only appear in a few recipes, where they are added whole, mainly for taste; these should be used cautiously. Dried fenugreek leaves are sold in Indian food stores. Store them in an airtight jar, in a cool, dark place; they will keep for about 12 months. Fenugreek seeds are small and pungent, and are widely used in spice mixtures.

Below: *Aromatic fresh fenugreek leaves are widely used in savoury Indian dishes.*

CURRY POWDERS and PASTES

Powders and pastes are blends of spices, chillies and herbs that are used as the basis of a curry. Traditional Indian households would blend individual spices as needed, but for convenience you may prefer to prepare a quantity in advance.

Curry powder

This is a basic recipe for a dry spice blend for use in any curry dish. It is a mild recipe, but you could increase the quantity of dried chilli for a hotter taste.

MAKES ABOUT 115G/4OZ/½ CUP

50g/2oz/½ cup coriander seeds
60ml/4 tbsp cumin seeds
30ml/2 tbsp fennel seeds
30ml/2 tbsp fenugreek seeds
4 dried red chillies
5 curry leaves
15ml/1 tbsp chilli powder
15ml/1 tbsp ground turmeric
2.5ml/½ tsp salt

1 Dry-roast the whole spices in a wok, karahi or large pan for 8–10 minutes, shaking the pan until the spices darken and release a rich aroma. Allow to cool.

2 Put the dry-roasted whole spices in a spice mill and grind to a fine powder.

3 Add the ground, roasted spices to the chilli powder, turmeric and salt in a large glass bowl and mix well. Store the curry powder in an airtight container.

Garam masala

Garam means hot and masala means spices, and this mixture uses spices that are known to heat the body, such as black peppercorns and cloves. Garam masala is used mainly for meat, although it can be used in poultry and rice dishes. The aroma is generally considered too strong for fish or vegetable dishes.

MAKES ABOUT 50G/2OZ/¼ CUP

10 dried red chillies
3 × 2.5cm/1in pieces cinnamon stick
2 curry leaves
30ml/2 tbsp coriander seeds
30ml/2 tbsp cumin seeds
5ml/1 tsp black peppercorns
5ml/1 tsp cloves
5ml/1 tsp fenugreek seeds
5ml/1 tsp black mustard seeds
1.5ml/¼ tsp chilli powder

1 Dry-roast the whole dried red chillies, cinnamon sticks and curry leaves in a wok, karahi or large pan over a low heat for about 2 minutes.

2 Add the coriander and cumin seeds, black peppercorns, cloves, fenugreek and mustard seeds, and dry-roast for 8–10 minutes, shaking the pan from side to side until the spices begin to darken in colour and release a rich aroma. Allow the mixture to cool.

3 Using either a spice mill or a stainless steel mortar and pestle, grind the roasted spices to a fine powder.

4 Transfer the powder to a glass bowl and mix in the chilli powder. Store in an airtight container.

COOK'S TIP

Both the curry powder and the garam masala will keep for 2–4 months in an airtight container in a cool, dark place. Once opened, store in the refrigerator.

VARIATIONS

For convenience, you can buy garam masala ready-made, or try any of the following pastes in alternative flavours:
• Tandoori masala
• Kashmiri masala
• Madras masala
• Sambhar masala
• Dhansak masala
• Green masala

Curry paste

A curry paste is a wet blend of spices, herbs and chillies cooked with oil and vinegar, which help to preserve the spices during storage. It is a quick and convenient way of adding a spice mixture to a curry, and different blends will produce different flavours. As only a small amount of paste is added at a time, a little will last a long time. Store in the refrigerator and use as required.

MAKES ABOUT 600ML/1 PINT/2½ CUPS

50g/2oz/½ cup coriander seeds
60ml/4 tbsp cumin seeds
30ml/2 tbsp fennel seeds
30ml/2 tbsp fenugreek seeds
4 dried red chillies
5 curry leaves
15ml/1 tbsp chilli powder
15ml/1 tbsp ground turmeric
150ml/¼ pint/⅔ cup wine vinegar
250ml/8fl oz/1 cup vegetable oil

1 Grind the whole spices to a powder in a spice mill. Transfer to a bowl and add the remaining ground spices.

2 Mix the spices until well blended. Add the wine vinegar and stir. Add 75ml/5 tbsp water and stir to form a paste.

3 Heat the oil in a wok, karahi or large pan and stir-fry the spice paste for about 10 minutes, or until all the water has been absorbed. When the oil rises to the surface the paste is cooked. Allow to cool slightly before spooning the paste into airtight jars.

COOK'S TIP

Once the paste has been cooked, heat a little more oil and pour on top of the paste in an airtight jar. This will help to preserve the paste and, as the oil stays on top as the paste is used, it will stop any mould from forming during storage. Store in the refrigerator.

Tikka paste

This is a delicious, versatile paste. It has a slightly sour flavour, and can be used in a variety of Indian dishes, including chicken tikka, tandoori chicken and tikka masala. Use sparingly as a little bit goes a long way. Store the paste in airtight glass jars in the refrigerator until required.

MAKES ABOUT 475ML/16FL OZ/2 CUPS

30ml/2 tbsp coriander seeds
30ml/2 tbsp cumin seeds
25ml/1½ tbsp garlic powder
30ml/2 tbsp paprika
15ml/1 tbsp garam masala
15ml/1 tbsp ground ginger
10ml/2 tsp chilli powder
2.5ml/½ tsp ground turmeric
15ml/1 tbsp dried mint
1.5ml/¼ tsp salt
5ml/1 tsp lemon juice
a few drops of red food colouring
a few drops of yellow food colouring
150ml/¼ pint/⅔ cup wine vinegar
150ml/¼ pint/⅔ cup vegetable oil

1 Grind the coriander and cumin seeds to a fine powder using a spice mill or mortar and pestle. Spoon the mixture into a bowl and add the remaining spices, the mint and salt, stirring well.

2 Mix the spice powder with the lemon juice, food colourings and wine vinegar and add 30ml/2 tbsp water to form a thin paste.

3 Heat the oil in a large pan, wok or karahi, and stir-fry the paste for 10 minutes, until all the water has been absorbed. When the oil rises to the surface, the paste is cooked. Allow to cool before spooning into airtight jars.

COOK'S TIP

Curry pastes will keep for 3–4 weeks after opening, if stored in the refrigerator.

ADDITIONAL INGREDIENTS

Besides the essential spices, aromatics and herbs, there are several other ingredients that are central to Indian cooking. Among the additional ingredients listed here are popular thickening and souring agents, flavourings and Indian cheese.

Above: Cashew nuts

Almonds

In the West, almonds are readily available whole, sliced, ground, and as thin slivers. The whole kernels should be soaked in boiling water before use to remove the thin red skin; once blanched, they can be eaten raw. Almonds have a uniqe aroma and they impart a sumptuous richness to curries. They make an effective thickener for sauces, and are also used for garnishing. Almonds are considered a delicacy in India and, because they are not indigenous, they are very expensive to buy.

Left: Whole almond kernels

Cashew nuts

These full-flavoured nuts can be used raw and roasted in Indian cooking. Cashews are ground and used in korma dishes to enrich and thicken the sauce, or they can also be toasted and sprinkled over pulaos and biryanis, as a garnish. In India, cashews are often used in vegetable and rice dishes as a substitute for the more expensive almonds.

Pistachio nuts

These small, greenish purple nuts are not indigenous to India, but they are frequently used as a thickening agent and to add their characteristic rich and creamy flavour. Raw or toasted pistachio nuts also make an attractive garnish.

Poppy seeds

These seeds are usually toasted to bring out their full, nutty flavour. They can be sprinkled over dry meat and vegetable dishes, or ground and added to curries to thicken sauces.

Sesame seeds

These small, flat, pear-shaped seeds probably originated in Africa but have been cultivated in India since ancient times. They are usually white but can be cream to brown, red or black. Raw sesame seeds have very little aroma and taste until they have been roasted or dry-fried, when they take on a slightly nutty taste. They can be ground with a mortar and pestle, or in a spice mill, and used to enrich curries. They are also added to chutneys. The high fat content of sesame seeds means that they do not keep well: buy them in small quantities and store in a cool, dark place.

Pomegranate seeds

These can be extracted from fresh pomegranates or, for convenience, they can be bought in jars from Asian food stores. Pomegranate seeds impart a delicious tangy flavour.

Dry mango powder

Mangoes are indigenous to India, and they have many uses in Indian cooking. The fruit is used in curries at different stages of ripeness, but the unripe fruit is also sun-dried and ground into a dry powder called *amchur*. The powder has a sour taste, and is sprinkled over dishes as a garnish; it is not used in cooking.

Above: White and black poppy seeds

Right: Black sesame seeds and white sesame seeds

Above: Fresh coconut

Coconut

Used in both sweet and savoury Indian dishes, fresh coconut is available from Indian food stores and supermarkets. Desiccated (dry, unsweetened, shredded) coconut, and coconut cream and creamed coconut, which are made from grated coconut, will all make acceptable substitutes in most recipes if fresh coconut is out of season. Coconut milk is used in Indian curries to thicken and enrich sauces. In Western supermarkets, it is sold in cans and in powdered form, as a convenient alternative to the fresh fruit; the powdered milk has to be blended with hot water before use. Coconut milk can be made at home from desiccated coconut. Coconut cream is used to add fragrance and aroma to dishes, while creamed coconut adds richness.

Below: Clockwise from left, coconut cream, coconut milk and desiccated coconut

MAKING COCONUT MILK

You can make as much of the milk as you like from this recipe by adapting the quantities accordingly, although the method is more practical for larger quantities.

Tip 225g/8oz/2⅔ cups desiccated (dry, unsweetened, shredded) coconut into a food processor and pour over 450ml/¾ pint/scant 2 cups boiling water. Process for 20–30 seconds, then cool. Place a sieve lined with muslin (cheesecloth) over a bowl in the sink. Ladle some of the softened coconut into the muslin. Bring up the ends of the cloth and twist it over the sieve to extract the liquid. Use the milk as directed in recipes. Coconut milk will keep for 1–2 days in the refrigerator, or it can be frozen for use on a later occasion.

Yogurt

In India, yogurt is known as curd. It can be added to sauces to give a thick and creamy texture, although it is most often used as a souring agent, particularly in the dairy-dominated north. Yogurt will curdle quickly when heated, and it should be used with care in recipes: add only a spoonful at a time, stir well and allow the sauce to simmer for five minutes before adding the next spoonful. In India, yogurt would be made at home on a daily basis, although ready-made natural (plain) yogurt is an acceptable substitute. Always choose live yogurt because of its beneficial effect on the digestive system.

Below: Fresh paneer

Paneer

This traditional North Indian cheese is made from rich dairy milk. Paneer is white in colour and smooth-textured. It is usually available from Indian food stores and large supermarkets, but tofu and beancurd are adequate substitutes.

MAKING PANEER

Paneer is very easy to make, and adventurous cooks may prefer to make their own at home.

Bring 1 litre/1¾ pints/4 cups milk to the boil over a low heat. Add 30ml/2 tbsp lemon juice, and stir gently until the milk thickens and begins to curdle. Strain the curdled milk through a sieve lined with muslin (cheesecloth). Set the curd aside for 1½–2 hours, under a heavy weight to press it into a flat shape, about 1cm/½in thick. Cut into wedges and use as required. Paneer will keep for up to 1 week in the refrigerator.

Tamarind

The brown fruit pods of the tamarind tree are 15–20cm/6–8in long. Inside, the seeds are surrounded by a sticky brown pulp. Tamarind is cultivated in India, as well as in other parts of South-east Asia, East Africa and the West Indies, and it is undoubtably one of the natural treasures of the East. The high tartaric acid content makes tamarind an excellent souring agent, and for this purpose it has no substitute. It doesn't have a strong aroma but the flavour is wonderful: tart without being bitter, fruity and refreshing. Tamarind is sold compressed in blocks, and dried in slices. Fresh tamarind and concentrate and paste are also available.

PREPARING COMPRESSED TAMARIND

Asian food stores and supermarkets sell compressed tamarind in a solid block, and in this form it looks rather like a packet of dried dates.

To prepare compressed tamarind, tear off a piece that is roughly equivalent to 15ml/1 tbsp. Put the tamarind in a jug (pitcher) and add 150ml/¼ pint/⅔ cup warm water. Leave to soak for 10 minutes. Swirl the tamarind around with your fingers so that the pulp is released from the seeds. Using a nylon sieve, strain the juice into a bowl. Discard the contents of the sieve, and use the liquid as required. Store any leftover liquid in the refrigerator for use in another recipe.

Below: Tamarind, compressed into a block

FRUITS

Indians love fruit and, as well as eating fresh fruits raw as a dessert at the end of a meal, they will also cook them with spices, chilli and coconut milk in savoury dishes. The exotic fruits listed here are all native to India, and they are as diverse in colour and shape as they are in flavour.

Mangoes

Ripe, fresh mangoes grow in India throughout the summer months, and are used in sweet dishes. Unripe green mangoes, sold in the springtime, are used to make tangy pickles and chutneys, and are added to curries as a souring agent for seasoning.

Papayas

Also known as pawpaw, these pear-shaped fruits are native to tropical America, and were not introduced to Asia until the 17th century. When ripe, the green skin turns a speckled yellow and the pulp is a vibrant orange-pink. The edible small black seeds taste peppery when dried. Peel off the skin using a sharp knife and eat the creamy flesh of the ripe fruit raw. The unripe green fruit is used in cooking: one of the unique properties of papaya is that it will help to tenderize meat.

Pineapples

These distinctive-looking fruits have a sweet, golden and exceedingly juicy flesh. Unlike most other fruits, pineapples do not ripen after picking, although leaving a slightly unripe fruit at room temperature will help to reduce its acidity. Pineapples are cultivated in India, mainly in the South, and are gently cooked with spices to make palate cleansing side dishes.

Bananas

The soft and creamy flesh of bananas is high in starch, and is an excellent source of energy. Indians use several varieties of banana in vegetarian curries, including plantains, green bananas, and the sweet red-skinned variety.

Lemons and limes

These citrus fruits are indigenous to India, although limes, which in India are confusingly called lemons, are the most commonly available of the two. Both fruits are used as souring agents and are added to curries at the end of the cooking process; adding them any sooner would prevent any meat in the dish from becoming tender while it cooks.

Above: Lemons (top) and limes are used as souring agents in Indian curries.

Above: A whole papaya, with the cut fruit showing the small black, edible seeds.

Right: Sweet, red-skinned bananas and the more familiar large and small yellow-skinned varieties.

VEGETABLES

Indian cooking specializes in a huge range of excellent vegetable dishes, using everything from cauliflower, potatoes and peas to the more exotic and unusual varieties, such as okra, bottle gourds and aubergines (eggplant). When it comes to Indian cooking, vegetables are simply indispensable.

Aubergines

Available in different varieties, the shiny deep purple aubergine is the most common and widely used variety in Indian cooking. Aubergines have a strong flavour and some have a slightly bitter taste. The cut flesh may be sprinkled with salt to extract these bitter juices.

Left: Small and large onions

Left: Various sizes of purple aubergines

Bottle gourds

One of the many bitter vegetables used in Indian cooking, this long, knobbly green vegetable comes from Kenya and has a strong, bitter taste. It is known to have properties that purify the blood.
To prepare a gourd, peel the ridged skin with a sharp knife, scrape away and discard the seeds and chop the flesh.

Okra

Also known as ladies' fingers, okra are one of the most popular vegetables in Indian cooking. These small green five-sided pods are indigenous to India. They have a very distinctive flavour and a sticky, pulpy texture when they are cooked.

Onions

A versatile vegetable belonging to the allium family, onions have a strong pungent flavour and aroma. Globe onions are the most commonly used variety for Indian cooking. Spring onions (scallions) are also used in some dishes to add colour and for their mild taste.

Peppers

Large, hollow pods belonging to the capsicum family, (bell) peppers are available in a variety of colours. Red peppers are sweeter than green peppers. They are used in a wide variety of dishes, adding both colour and flavour.

Spinach

Available all year round, this leafy green vegetable has a mild, delicate flavour. The leaves vary in size and only the large thick leaves need to be trimmed of their stalks. Spinach is a favourite vegetable in Indian cooking, and it is cooked in many ways, with meat, other vegetables, and with beans, peas and lentils.

Corn

Although it originated in South America, corn is now grown worldwide, and is grown extensively in North India. It has a delicious sweet, juicy flavour, which is at its best just after picking.

Tomatoes

These are an essential ingredient, and are used to make sauces for curries, chutneys and relishes. Salad tomatoes are quite adequate but are usually peeled. Use canned tomatoes in sauces and curries for their rich colour.

Above: Peppers

BEANS, PEAS and LENTILS

These play an important role in Indian cooking and are an excellent source of protein and fibre. Some are cooked whole, some are puréed and made into soups or dhals, and some are combined with vegetables or meat. Beans and chickpeas should be soaked before cooking. Lentils do not need to be soaked. Red and green split lentils cook to a soft consistency, and whole lentils hold their shape when cooked.

Black-eyed beans
These are small and cream-coloured, with a black spot or "eye". When cooked, black-eyed beans (peas) have a tender, creamy texture and a mild, smoky flavour. They are used widely in Indian cooking.

PREPARING AND COOKING BEANS AND PEAS
Beans and chickpeas should be boiled for at least 10 minutes before cooking to destroy the potentially harmful toxins that they contain.

Wash the beans or chickpeas under cold running water, then place in a large bowl of fresh cold water and leave to soak overnight. Discard any pulses that float to the surface, drain and rinse again. Put in a large pan and cover with plenty of fresh cold water. Bring to the boil and boil rapidly for 10–15 minutes. Reduce the heat and simmer until tender. Drain and use as required.

Above: Chickpeas

Chana dhal
This round, yellow split lentil is similar in appearance to the yellow split pea, which will make a good substitute. It is cooked in a variety of vegetable dishes and can be deep-fried and mixed with spices for the Indian snack Bombay mix. Chana dhal is often used as a binding agent in Indian curries.

Chickpeas
These round, beige-coloured pulses have a strong, nutty flavour when cooked. As well as being used for curries, they are also ground into a flour that is widely used in many Indian dishes, such as pakoras and bhajiyas, and are also added to Indian snacks.

Left: From left, haricot (navy) beans, red kidney beans and pinto beans

Flageolet beans
These white or pale green oval beans have a very mild, refreshing flavour.

Green lentils
Also known as continental lentils, these have a strong flavour and they retain their shape during cooking.

Haricot beans
These small, white oval beans come in different varieties. Known as navy in the United States, these beans are ideal for Indian cooking because they retain their shape and absorb flavours.

Kidney beans
These red-brown kidney-shaped beans have a distinctive flavour. They belong to the same family as the pinto bean.

Mung beans
These small, round green beans have a sweet flavour and creamy texture. When sprouted, mung beans produce beansprouts. Split mung beans are also used, and are often cooked with rice.

Red split lentils
Another lentil that can be used for making dhal. Use instead of tuvar dhal.

Tuvar dhal
A dull orange-coloured split pea with a distinctive earthy flavour. Tuvar dhal is available plain and in an oily variety.

Urid dhal
This lentil is available split, either with the blackish hull retained or removed. It has quite a dry texture when cooked.

Above: Red lentils

RICE

This staple grain is served with almost every meal in some parts of India, so it is no surprise that the Indians have created a variety of ways of cooking it, each quite distinctive. Plain boiled rice is an everyday accompaniment; for special occasions and entertaining, it is often combined with other ingredients.

There is no definitive way to cook plain rice, but whatever the recipe, the aim is to produce dry, separate-grained rice that is cooked through yet still retains some bite. The secret is the amount of water added: the rice must be able to absorb it all.

Basmati rice

Known as the prince of rices, basmati is the recommended rice for Indian curries – not only because it is easy to cook and produces an excellent finished result, but because it has a cooling effect on hot and spicy curries. Basmati is a slender, long grain, milled rice grown in northern India, the Punjab, parts of Pakistan and in the foothills of the Himalayas. Its name means fragrant, and it has a distinctive and appealing aroma. After harvesting it is aged for a year, which gives it the characteristic flavour and a light, fluffy texture. Basmati can be used in almost any savoury dish, particularly curries or pilaus, and is the essential ingredient in biryanis. White and brown basmati rices are widely available from supermarkets and Indian food stores.

Above: White basmati, probably the most commonly eaten rice in India.

COOKING PLAIN BOILED RICE

Always make sure you use a tight-fitting lid for your rice pan. If you do not have a lid that fits tightly, you can either wrap a dishtowel around the lid or put some foil between the lid and the pan to make a snug fit. Try not to remove the lid until the rice is cooked. (The advantage of using just a lid is that you can tell when the rice is ready because steam begins to escape, visibly and rapidly.)

As a rough guide, allow 75g/3oz/ scant ½ cup rice per person.

1 Put the dry rice in a colander and rinse it under cold running water until the water runs clear.

2 Place the rice in a large, deep pan and pour in enough cold water to come 2cm/¾in above the surface of the rice. Add a pinch of salt and, if you like, 5ml/1 tsp vegetable oil, stir once and bring to the boil.

3 Stir once more, reduce the heat to the lowest possible setting and cover the pan with a tight-fitting lid.

4 Cook the rice for 12–15 minutes, then turn off the heat and leave the rice to stand, still tightly covered, for about 10 minutes.

5 Before serving, gently fluff up the rice with a fork or slotted rice spoon – the slotted spoon will prevent you from breaking up the grains, which would make the rice mushy.

Below: Patna rice, a long grain rice native to eastern India.

Patna rice

This rice takes its name from Patna in eastern India. At one time, most of the long grain rice sold in Europe came from Patna, and the term was used loosely to mean any long grain rice, whatever its origin. The custom still persists in parts of the United States, but elsewhere Patna is used to describe the specific variety of rice grown in the eastern state of Bihar. Patna rice is used in the same way as other long grain rices, and is suitable for use wherever plain boiled rice is called for.

BREADS

Breads are an integral part of any Indian meal. Most traditional Indian breads are unleavened, that is, made without any raising agent, and are made with wholemeal (wholewheat) flour, known as chapati flour or atta.

Throughout India, breads vary from region to region, depending on local ingredients. Some breads are cooked dry on a hot griddle, while some are fried with a little oil, and others are deep-fried to make small savoury puffs. To enjoy Indian breads at their best they should be made just before you are ready to serve the meal, so that they can be eaten hot.

Naan

Probably the most well-known Indian bread outside India is naan, from the north of the country. Naan is made with plain (all-purpose) flour, yogurt and yeast; some contemporary recipes favour the use of a chemical raising agent such as bicarbonate of soda (baking soda) or self-raising (self-rising) flour as a leaven in place of yeast. The yogurt is important for the fermentation of the dough, and some naan are made entirely using a yogurt fermentation. Fermentation gives the bread its characteristic light, puffy texture and soft crust. The flavour comes partly from the soured yogurt and partly from the *tandoor*, which is the the clay oven, sunk into the ground, in which the bread is traditionally cooked. The bread is flattened against the blisteringly hot walls of the oven and the pull of gravity produces the characteristic teardrop shape. As the dough scorches and puffs up, it produces a bread that is soft and crisp. Naan can be eaten with almost any meat or vegetable dish. There are many types of flavoured naan sold commercially, including plain, coriander (cilantro) and garlic, and masala naan.

Chapatis

The favourite bread of central and southern India is the chapati, a thin, flat, unleavened bread made from ground

Above: Chapatis and parathas

Below: Poppadums

wholemeal flour. Chapatis are cooked on a hot *tava*, a concave-shaped Indian griddle. Chapatis have a light texture and fairly bland flavour, which makes them an ideal accompaniment for highly spiced curry dishes. Spices can be added to the flour to give more flavour.

Rotis

There are many variations of chapatis, including *rotis* and *dana rotis*. These are unleavened breads, made using chapati flour to which ghee, oil, celery seeds and/or fresh coriander are added. They are rolled out thinly and cooked like chapatis.

Parathas

A paratha is similar to a chapati except that it contains ghee (clarified butter), which gives the bread a richer flavour and flakier texture. Parathas are much thicker than chapatis and are shallow-fried. Plain parathas are often eaten for lunch, and they go well with most vegetable dishes. They can be stuffed with various fillings, the most popular being spiced potato. Stuffed parathas are served as a snack.

Pooris

Another popular variation on the chapati is the poori, which is a small, deep-fried puffy bread made from chapati flour. Pooris are best eaten sizzling hot and are traditionally served for breakfast. They can be plain or flavoured with spices, such as cumin, turmeric and chilli powder, which are mixed into the dough. Pooris are often served with fish or vegetable curries.

Poppadums

These are now widely available outside of India. These are large, thin crisp disks, which can be bought ready-cooked or ready-to-cook. In India they are served with vegetarian meals. They are sold in markets and by street vendors, and are available plain or flavoured with spices or seasoned with ground red or black pepper. The dough is generally made from dried beans, but can also be made from potatoes or sago. It is thinly rolled and left to dry in the sun. Poppadums are cooked either by deep-frying or placing under a hot grill (broiler).

Above: Naan

EQUIPMENT and UTENSILS

While a reasonably stocked kitchen will provide most of the equipment needed for cooking Indian curries, it may still be necessary to invest in one or two more specialist items to ensure perfect results.

Chapati griddle
Known in India as a *tava*, the chapati griddle allows chapatis and other breads to be cooked without burning. The heavy wrought-iron frying pan can also be used to dry-roast spices. Traditionally, the griddle would be set over an open fire but it will work equally well on a gas flame or electric hob.

Chapati rolling board
This round wooden board on short stubby legs is used to mould breads into shape; the extra height provided by the legs helps to disperse excess dry flour. A wooden pastry board makes an appropriate substitute.

Chapati rolling pin
The traditional chapati rolling pin is thinner in shape than Western rolling pins, and comes in many different sizes. Use whichever size feels the most comfortable in your hands.

Heat diffuser
Many curries are left to simmer slowly over a low heat, and a heat diffuser will help to prevent burning on the base of the karahi or wok.

Grinding stone and pin
The traditional oblong grinding stone is the Indian equivalent of the Western food processor. Fresh and dry ingredients are placed on the heavy slate stone, which is marked with notches to hold ingredients in place. The ingredients are then pulverized against the stone, using the heavy rolling pin.

Above: Chapati griddle and chapati rolling pin

Left: Grinding stone and rolling pin, tongs and stainless steel mortar and pestle

Below right: Heat diffuser

Table sizzler
This heated appliance allows food that is still cooking to be brought to the dinner table ready for serving. It is very useful for entertaining.

Slotted spoon
Stirring cooked, drained rice with a slotted spoon will make the rice soft, fluffy by allowing air in between the grains; the slots in the spoon prevent the grains from breaking as the rice is moved around the pan. The spoon also used to remove foods from hot oil or other cooking liquids.

Chapati spoon
The square, flat-headed chapati spoon is used for turning roasting breads on the hot chapati griddle. A fish slice (spatula) may also be used.

Spice mill
An electric spice mill is useful for grinding small quantities of

Below:
A traditional
cast-iron karahi

Karahi

Basically an Indian frying pan, the karahi, is similar to a wok but is more rounded in shape and is made of heavier metal: originally, the karahi would be made of cast iron, although a variety of metals are now used. Karahis are available in various sizes, including small ones for cooking single portions. Serving food from a karahi at the table adds an authentic touch to the meal.

Wok

This is a good substitute for a karahi for cooking most types of Indian dish. Buy the appropriate wok for your cooker. Round-bottomed woks can be used on gas hobs only; flat-bottomed woks are for use on electric hobs.

Stainless steel pans

Quality kitchen pans in various sizes are essential for cooking rice, vegetables and other ingredients. A heavy-based non-stick frying pan can be used in place of a karahi or wok.

Above: Stainless steel pans

ingredients such as spices. A coffee grinder – used solely for this purpose, as it will retain the strong smell of the spices – would make a good substitute.

Stainless steel mortar and pestle

These are ideal for grinding small amounts of wet ingredients, such as fresh root ginger, chillies and garlic. Stainless steel is everlasting and will not retain the strong flavours of the spices.

Stone mortar and pestle

A heavy granite mortar and pestle is traditionally used to grind small amounts of ingredients, both wet and dry.

Pastry brush

Use for brushing and basting meats and vegetables lightly with oil before and during grilling (broiling).

Balloon whisk

A metal whisk is useful for beating yogurt and dairy or coconut cream before adding to recipes.

Knives

Kitchen knives in a range of sizes are essential. Keep knives sharp to make it easier to chop ingredients and to ensure neat edges when cutting.

Colander and sieve

Use for draining boiled rice and vegetables, and for straining ingredients. Choose a long-handled, sturdy colander and sieve made from stainless steel, as these allow you to stand back to pour steaming rice out of a pan, and will not discolour like plastic ones.

Food processor

This is essential for blending the ingredients. Smaller quantities can be ground in a mortar and pestle.

Right: From left, stainless steel colander and sieve

NORTH INDIA

The cuisine of northern India has been heavily influenced by a great

many foreign settlers, traders and pilgrims. The most notable of these

were the Moguls, who added Mughlai food and a selection of exotic

fruit and nuts to the established traditions of Kashmir and Punjab.

KASHMIRI CHICKEN CURRY

Surrounded by the snow-capped Himalayas, Kashmir is popularly known as the "Switzerland of the East". The state is also renowned for its rich culinary heritage, and this aromatic dish is one of the simplest among the region's repertoire.

2 Rub the chicken pieces with the marinade and allow to rest in a cool place for a further 2 hours, or in the refrigerator overnight. Bring to room temperature before cooking.

3 Heat the oil in a wok, karahi or large pan and fry half the ginger and all the garlic until golden. Add the chicken and fry until both sides are sealed. Cover and cook until the chicken is tender, and the oil has separated from the sauce.

SERVES 4–6

20ml/4 tsp Kashmiri masala paste
60ml/4 tbsp tomato ketchup
5ml/1 tsp Worcestershire sauce
5ml/1 tsp five-spice powder
5ml/1 tsp granulated sugar
8 chicken joints, skinned
45ml/3 tbsp vegetable oil
5cm/2in piece fresh root ginger, finely shredded
4 garlic cloves, crushed
juice of 1 lemon
15ml/1 tbsp coriander (cilantro) leaves, finely chopped
salt

1 To make the marinade, mix the masala paste, tomato ketchup, Worcestershire sauce, five-spice powder, salt and sugar. Allow the mixture to rest in a warm place until the sugar has dissolved.

4 Sprinkle the chicken with the lemon juice, remaining ginger and chopped coriander leaves, and mix in well. Serve hot. Plain boiled rice would make a good accompaniment.

TANDOORI CHICKEN

Punjab, in northern India, is the home of tandoori food. The tandoor, or clay oven,
originated in Egypt and found its way into India with the Moguls. It is probably the most
versatile oven in the world, capable of roasting, grilling and baking all at the same time.

SERVES 4–6

1.3kg/3lb oven-ready chicken
250ml/8fl oz/1 cup natural (plain)
  yogurt, beaten
60ml/4 tbsp tandoori masala paste
75g/3oz/2 tbsp ghee or vegetable oil
salt
lemon slice and onion rings, to garnish
lettuce, to serve

1 Using a small, sharp knife or scissors, remove the skin from the chicken and trim off any excess fat. Using a fork, prick the flesh at random.

2 Cut the chicken in half down the centre and through the breast. Cut each piece in half again. Make a few deep gashes diagonally into the flesh.

3 Mix the yogurt with the masala paste and season with salt. Spread the chicken with the yogurt mixture, spreading some into the gashes. Leave to marinate in a cool place for at least 2 hours, or in the refrigerator overnight.

4 Preheat the oven to 240°C/475°F/ Gas 9. Place the chicken quarters on a wire rack in a deep baking tray. Spread the chicken with any excess marinade, reserving a little for basting halfway through the cooking time.

COOK'S TIP
If the chicken is left overnight in the refrigerator, remove it a hour or two before you want to start cooking to allow it to return to room temperature.

5 Melt the ghee and pour over the chicken pieces to seal the surface. This helps to keep the centre moist during roasting. Roast the chicken for about 10 minutes, then remove from the oven, leaving the oven on.

6 Baste the chicken with the remaining marinade. Return to the oven and switch off the heat. Leave the chicken in the oven for 15–20 minutes without opening the door. Serve on a bed of lettuce and garnish with the lemon and onion rings.

KARAHI CHICKEN with MINT

A karahi is similar to a Chinese wok, and its use is most widespread in northern India, which is closest to the border with China. A traditional karahi is made of heavy cast iron, which is excellent for heat distribution and retention, and it is used extensively for cooking all types of meat, poultry and vegetable dishes. Because of its shape, it is also ideal for deep-frying and is used for this purpose all over India.

2 Heat the oil in a large pan, add the chopped spring onions and stir-fry for about 2 minutes until soft.

3 Add the boiled chicken strips to the pan and stir-fry briskly over a medium heat for about 3 minutes, or until the chicken is browned.

4 Add the grated fresh root ginger, chilli, lemon juice, chopped coriander and mint, tomatoes and salt, and stir gently to blend the flavours.

5 Transfer the curry to a warmed serving platter and garnish with fresh coriander and mint sprigs before serving. Plain boiled rice would make a good accompaniment to this dish.

VARIATION

Use strips of turkey breast meat or pork tenderloin instead of chicken. If using, pork tenderloin, flatten the meat with a steak mallet first to tenderize it, then cut into strips and use as directed.

SERVES 4

450g/1lb chicken breast fillets, skinned and
    cut into strips
300ml/½ pint/1¼ cups water
30ml/2 tbsp vegetable oil
2 small bunches spring onions
    (scallions), roughly chopped
5ml/1 tsp grated fresh root ginger
5ml/1 tsp crushed dried red chilli
30ml/2 tbsp lemon juice
30ml/2 tbsp chopped fresh coriander
    (cilantro), plus extra sprigs to garnish
30ml/2 tbsp chopped fresh mint, plus extra
    sprigs to garnish
3 tomatoes, seeded and roughly chopped
5ml/1 tsp salt

1 Put the chicken and water into a large pan, bring to the boil and lower the heat to medium. Cook for about 10 minutes or until the water has evaporated and the chicken is cooked. Remove the pan from the heat and set aside.

KARAHI CHICKEN with FRESH FENUGREEK

This karahi chicken was the dish that inspired a style of cooking known as karahi cuisine in northern India, where fenugreek is a typical flavouring agent. In the West, dried fenugreek leaves can be used for convenience, as fresh fenugreek is generally more difficult to find. The dried leaves are sold in Indian and Pakistani food stores throughout the year, and will keep well in an airtight jar.

SERVES 4

225g/8oz chicken thigh meat, skinned
    and cut into strips
225g/8oz chicken breast fillets, skinned
    and cut into strips
2.5ml/½ tsp crushed garlic
5ml/1 tsp chilli powder
2.5ml/½ tsp salt
10ml/2 tsp tomato purée (paste)
30ml/2 tbsp vegetable oil
1 bunch fresh fenugreek leaves or
    15ml/1 tbsp dried
15ml/1 tbsp chopped fresh coriander
    (cilantro)

1 Bring a large pan of water to the boil, add the chicken strips and cook for 5–7 minutes. Drain and set aside.

2 In a bowl, combine the garlic, chilli powder and salt with the tomato purée.

COOK'S TIP
Discard the stems of fresh fenugreek, as they will impart a bitter flavour to the dish.

3 Heat the oil in a wok, karahi or large pan. Lower the heat and add the tomato purée and spice mixture.

4 Add the chicken pieces and stir-fry for 5–7 minutes. Lower the heat further.

5 Add the fenugreek leaves and the chopped fresh coriander to the pan. Continue to stir-fry for 5–7 minutes, then pour in 300ml/½ pint/1¼ cups water, cover and cook for a further 5 minutes. Serve hot.

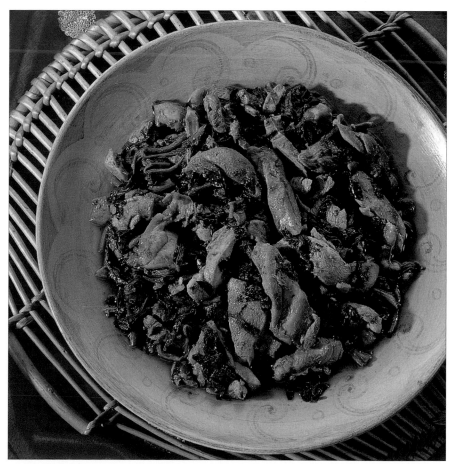

CHICKEN TIKKA MASALA

Though chicken tikka is a traditional dish from northern India, masala *is pure invention. The word refers to the sauce in which the cooked tikka is simmered and which is a western adaptation. However, it is not dissimilar to another traditional Indian dish known as butter chicken, in which cooked tandoori chicken is simmered in a creamy sauce.*

SERVES 4

675g/1½lb chicken breast fillets, skinned
90ml/6 tbsp tikka paste
60ml/4 tbsp natural (plain) yogurt
30ml/2 tbsp vegetable oil
1 onion, chopped
1 garlic clove, crushed
1 fresh green chilli, seeded and chopped
2.5cm/1in piece fresh root ginger, grated
15ml/1 tbsp tomato purée (paste)
15ml/1 tbsp ground almonds
250ml/8fl oz/1 cup water
45ml/3 tbsp ghee or butter, melted
50ml/2fl oz/¼ cup double (heavy) cream
15ml/1 tbsp lemon juice
fresh coriander (cilantro) sprigs, natural (plain) yogurt and toasted cumin seeds to garnish
naan bread, to serve

1 Cut the chicken into 2.5cm/1in cubes. Put half of the tikka paste and the yogurt into a bowl, then stir in the chicken. Leave to marinate for 20 minutes.

COOK'S TIP
Soak wooden kebab skewers in water before use to prevent them from burning while under the grill (broiler).

2 For the tikka sauce, heat the oil and fry the onion, garlic, chilli and ginger for 5 minutes. Add the remaining tikka paste and fry for 2 minutes. Add the tomato purée, almonds and water, and simmer for 15 minutes.

3 Thread the chicken on to wooden kebab skewers. Preheat the grill (broiler).

4 Brush the chicken pieces with the melted butter and grill (broil) under a medium heat for about 15 minutes. Occasionally, turn and brush the chicken pieces with more butter.

5 Put the tikka sauce in a blender or food processor and process until smooth. Return the sauce to the pan and stir in the cream and lemon juice.

6 Remove the chicken from the grill, slide the cubes off the wooden skewers and add them to the pan. Simmer gently for 5 minutes more. Garnish with fresh coriander, yogurt and cumin seeds, and serve with warm naan bread.

CHICKEN TIKKA

The word tikka *refers to the use of boneless, skinless cubes of chicken breast. Strictly speaking, the term cannot be applied to other types of meat, even if they are prepared and cooked in a similar way. Traditionally cooked in the tandoor (Indian clay oven), chicken tikka is enduringly popular in the West as well as in India.*

SERVES 6

450g/1lb chicken breast fillets, skinned, and cubed
5ml/1 tsp grated fresh root ginger
5ml/1 tsp crushed garlic
5ml/1 tsp chilli powder
1.5ml/¼ tsp ground turmeric
5ml/1 tsp salt
150ml/¼ pint/⅔ cup natural (plain) yogurt
60ml/4 tbsp lemon juice
15ml/1 tbsp chopped fresh coriander (cilantro)
15ml/1 tbsp vegetable oil

To serve (optional)
lettuce
1 small onion, cut into rings
lime wedges
fresh coriander (cilantro)

1 In a large bowl, mix the chicken cubes, ginger, garlic, chilli powder, turmeric, salt, yogurt, lemon juice and coriander. Leave to marinate in a cool place for at least 2 hours, or in the refrigerator overnight.

COOK'S TIP
Thread the meat on to oiled skewers, and turn and baste it during cooking.

2 Place the chicken on a grill (broiler) tray, or in a flameproof dish lined with foil, and baste with the oil.

3 Preheat the grill to medium. Grill (broil) the chicken for 15–20 minutes until cooked, turning and basting two or three times. Serve with lettuce, onion rings, lime wedges and fresh coriander.

CHICKEN SAAG

The word saag *means greens and, traditionally, spinach is the usual choice for adding to meat and poultry, although other greens also work well. Chicken saag is one of the best-known dishes to have originated in the state of Punjab.*

SERVES 4

225g/8oz fresh spinach leaves, washed
2.5cm/1in piece fresh root ginger, grated
2 garlic cloves, crushed
1 fresh green chilli, roughly chopped
200ml/7fl oz/scant 1 cup water
30ml/2 tbsp vegetable oil
2 bay leaves
1.5ml/¼ tsp black peppercorns
1 onion, finely chopped
4 tomatoes, skinned and
    finely chopped
10ml/2 tsp curry powder
5ml/1 tsp salt
5ml/1 tsp chilli powder
45ml/3 tbsp natural (plain) yogurt,
    plus extra to serve
8 chicken thighs, skinned
naan bread, to serve

1 Cook the spinach, without water, in a tightly covered pan for 5 minutes. Put the spinach, ginger, garlic and chilli with 50ml/2fl oz/¼ cup of the water into a food processor and process to a purée.

2 Heat the oil, add the bay leaves and peppercorns and fry for 2 minutes. Add the onion and fry for 6–8 minutes more.

3 Add the chopped tomatoes to the pan and simmer for a further 5 minutes. Add the curry powder, salt and chilli powder and stir well to mix. Allow to cook for 2 minutes.

4 Add the spinach purée and the remaining water to the pan, and leave to simmer for 5 minutes.

5 Stir in the yogurt, about 15ml/1 tbsp at a time, and simmer for 5 minutes.

6 Add the chicken. Cover and cook for 25–30 minutes or until the chicken is tender. Serve with warm naan, drizzle over some natural yogurt and dust lightly with the chilli powder.

CHICKEN in GREEN MASALA SAUCE

The use of green spice mixes is popular all over India. Although in southern India the mixes are generally used to cook vegetables and fish, in the north, where most people are meat-eaters, they are more often used to prepare meat and poultry dishes.

SERVES 4

1 crisp green eating apple, peeled, cored and cubed
60ml/4 tbsp fresh coriander (cilantro) leaves
30ml/2 tbsp fresh mint leaves
150ml/¼ pint/⅔ cup natural (plain) yogurt
45ml/3 tbsp fromage frais or ricotta cheese
2 fresh green chillies, seeded and chopped
1 bunch spring onions (scallions), chopped
5ml/1 tsp salt
5ml/1 tsp granulated sugar
5ml/1 tsp crushed garlic
5ml/1 tsp grated fresh root ginger
15ml/1 tbsp vegetable oil
225g/8oz chicken breast fillets, skinned and cubed
25g/1oz sultanas (golden raisins)

1 Place the apple, 45ml/3 tbsp of the coriander, the mint, yogurt, fromage frais or ricotta, chillies, spring onions, salt, sugar, garlic and ginger in a food processor and process for 1 minute. Scrape around the outside of the bowl and process for a few seconds more.

2 Heat the oil in a wok, karahi or large pan, pour in the yogurt mixture and cook gently over a low heat for about 2 minutes.

COOK'S TIP
This dish makes a good dinner-party main course. Nut Pulao would make a good accompaniment.

3 Add the chicken pieces and stir well to blend everything together. Cook over a medium-low heat for 12–15 minutes or until the chicken is fully cooked.

4 Sprinkle the sultanas and the remaining coriander over the chicken (do not mix in, but leave as a garnish). Serve with Nut Pulao, if you like.

SPICY GRILLED CHICKEN

This dish is inspired by the tandoori style of cooking, in which the meat and poultry are marinated before being grilled or roasted in a clay oven. Serve it with rice and a salad, or, for a real treat, with a mushroom curry.

SERVES 6

12 chicken thighs
90ml/6 tbsp lemon juice
5ml/1 tsp grated fresh root ginger
5ml/1 tsp crushed garlic
5ml/1 tsp crushed dried red chillies
5ml/1 tsp salt
5ml/1 tsp soft light brown sugar
30ml/2 tbsp clear honey
30ml/2 tbsp chopped fresh coriander
    (cilantro), plus extra sprigs
    to garnish
1 fresh green chilli, finely chopped
30ml/2 tbsp vegetable oil
Saffron Rice and a mixed salad,
    to serve (optional)

1 Prick the chicken thighs with a fork, rinse under running water, pat dry with kitchen paper and set aside.

2 In a bowl, mix the lemon juice, ginger, garlic, red chillies, salt, sugar and honey.

3 Transfer the chicken thighs to the spice mixture in the bowl and coat well. Leave to marinate for 45 minutes.

4 Preheat the grill (broiler) to medium. Add the fresh coriander and chopped green chilli to the chicken and mix well, then transfer the marinated chicken thighs to a flameproof dish.

5 Pour any remaining marinade over the chicken and baste with the oil, using a pastry brush.

6 Grill (broil) the chicken thighs for 15–20 minutes, turning and basting the meat occasionally, until cooked through and browned.

7 Transfer the chicken to a warmed serving dish and garnish with the fresh coriander sprigs. Serve with Saffron Rice and a salad, if you like.

COOK'S TIP
If you prefer, you can cook the chicken on a barbecue for a wonderful smoky flavour. Baste with the oil only when the chicken is almost cooked.

CHICKEN in a CASHEW NUT SAUCE

Nut pastes were introduced into north Indian cooking by the Moguls, the travellers who provided what was probably the most important outside influence on Indian cuisine. Mughlai food, as this style of cooking is known, is famed for its rich yet delicate flavours.

SERVES 4

2 onions
30ml/2 tbsp tomato purée (paste)
50g/2oz/⅓ cup cashew nuts
7.5ml/1½ tsp garam masala
5ml/1 tsp crushed garlic
5ml/1 tsp chilli powder
15ml/1 tbsp lemon juice
1.5ml/¼ tsp ground turmeric
5ml/1 tsp salt
15ml/1 tbsp natural (plain) yogurt
30ml/2 tbsp vegetable oil
15ml/1 tbsp chopped fresh coriander
   (cilantro), plus extra
   to garnish
15ml/1 tbsp sultanas (golden raisins)
450g/1lb chicken breast fillets, skinned
   and cubed
175g/6oz button (white) mushrooms
300ml/½ pint/1¼ cups water

1 Cut the onions into quarters, then place in a food processor or blender. Process for 1 minute.

2 Add the tomato purée, cashew nuts, garam masala, crushed garlic, chilli powder, lemon juice, turmeric, salt and yogurt to the onions and process for a further 1–1½ minutes.

3 In a wok, karahi or large pan, heat the oil, lower the heat to medium and pour in the onion and spice mixture from the food processor or blender. Fry gently, stirring frequently, for about 2 minutes, lowering the heat if necessary.

4 Add the fresh coriander, sultanas and cubed chicken to the pan and continue to stir-fry for a further minute.

5 Add the mushrooms, pour in the measured water and bring to a simmer. Cover the pan and cook over a low heat for about 10 minutes.

6 After this time, check that the chicken is cooked all the way through and the sauce is thick. Continue to cook for a little longer if necessary.

7 Transfer to a warmed serving dish and garnish with chopped fresh coriander. Plain boiled rice and a fruit chutney would go well with this dish.

CHICKEN DOPIAZA

With lashings of onions, dopiaza's popularity is timeless. The origin of the word is rather unclear. In the Hindi language Do means two and piaz is onion. Hence the popular belief that the word refers to the use of twice the amount or two different types of onions. However, dopiaza is essentially a Mogul dish and history has it that it was named after Emperor Akbar's courtier, Mullah Dopiaza.

SERVES 4

45ml/3 tbsp vegetable oil
8 small onions, halved
2 bay leaves
8 green cardamom pods
4 cloves
3 dried red chillies
8 black peppercorns
2 onions, finely chopped
2 garlic cloves, crushed
2.5cm/1in piece fresh root ginger,
   finely chopped
5ml/1 tsp ground coriander
5ml/1 tsp ground cumin
2.5ml/½ tsp ground turmeric
5ml/1 tsp chilli powder
2.5ml/½ tsp salt
4 tomatoes, skinned and finely chopped
120ml/4fl oz/½ cup water
8 chicken pieces, skinned
plain boiled rice or chapatis, to serve

1 Heat 30ml/2 tbsp oil in a wok, karahi or large pan and fry the halved small onions until soft. Remove and set aside.

2 Add the remaining oil and fry the bay leaves, cardamoms, cloves, chillies and peppercorns for 2 minutes. Add the chopped onions, garlic and ginger and fry for 5 minutes. Add the spices and salt and cook for 2 minutes.

COOK'S TIP
Soak the onions in boiling water for 2 minutes to make them easier to peel.

3 Add the tomatoes and water to the pan and simmer for 5 minutes until the sauce begins to thicken. Add the chicken pieces and cook for 15 minutes more.

4 Add the reserved small onions, then cover and cook for a further 10 minutes, or until the chicken is tender. Serve with plain boiled rice or chapatis.

CHICKEN KORMA

Korma is not really a dish but a technique employed in Indian cooking; it simply means braising. It is a misconception to think that kormas are always rich and creamy as there are several different types. They can be light and aromatic or rich and creamy, and some are fiery looking, with a taste to match. All depends on where the recipe originated. This recipe comes from Delhi, the centre of Mogul cuisine.

SERVES 4

25g/1oz blanched almonds
2 garlic cloves, crushed
2.5cm/1in piece fresh root ginger, chopped
30ml/2 tbsp vegetable oil
675g/1½lb chicken breast fillets, skinned
   and cubed
3 green cardamom pods
1 onion, finely chopped
10ml/2 tsp ground cumin
1.5ml/¼ tsp salt
150ml/¼ pint/⅔ cup natural (plain) yogurt
175ml/6fl oz/¾ cup single (light) cream
toasted flaked (sliced) almonds and fresh
   coriander (cilantro) sprigs, to garnish
plain boiled rice, to serve

1 Process the almonds, garlic and ginger in a food processor with 30ml/2 tbsp water.

2 Heat the oil in a wok, karahi or large pan, and cook the chicken for 10 minutes. Remove the chicken and set aside. Add the cardamom pods and fry for 2 minutes. Add the onion and fry for 5 minutes.

3 Stir the almond, garlic and ginger paste into the cardamom and onions in the pan. Add the cumin and season to taste with salt. Cook for 5 minutes more, stirring frequently.

4 Whisk the yogurt and add it to the onion mixture a tablespoonful at a time. Cook over a low heat, until the yogurt has all been absorbed. Return the chicken to the pan. Cover and simmer over a low heat for 5–6 minutes, or until the chicken is tender.

5 Stir in the cream and simmer for a further 5 minutes. Garnish with toasted flaked almonds and coriander, and serve with plain boiled rice.

COOK'S TIP
For a true Mogul flavour, replace the cumin with 15ml/1 tbsp ground coriander.

LAHORE-STYLE LAMB

Named after the city of Lahore, which has been in Pakistan since the Independence, this hearty dish has a wonderfully aromatic flavour imparted by the winter spices such as cloves, black peppercorns and cinnamon. Serve with a hot puffy naan in true north Indian style.

SERVES 4

60ml/4 tbsp vegetable oil
1 bay leaf
2 cloves
4 black peppercorns
1 onion, sliced
450g/1lb lean lamb, boned and cubed
1.5ml/¼ tsp ground turmeric
7.5ml/1½ tsp chilli powder
5ml/1 tsp crushed coriander seeds
2.5cm/1in piece cinnamon stick
5ml/1 tsp crushed garlic
7.5ml/1½ tsp salt
1.5 litres/2½ pints/6¼ cups water
50g/2oz/⅓ cup chana dhal or yellow
    split peas
2 tomatoes, quartered
2 fresh green chillies, chopped
15ml/1 tbsp chopped fresh coriander
    (cilantro)

1 Heat the oil in a wok, karahi or large pan. Lower the heat slightly and add the bay leaf, cloves, peppercorns and onion. Fry for about 5 minutes, or until the onion is golden brown.

2 Add the cubed lamb, turmeric, chilli powder, coriander seeds, cinnamon stick, garlic and most of the salt, and stir-fry for about 5 minutes over a medium heat.

3 Pour in 900ml/1½ pints/3¾ cups of the water and cover the pan with a lid or foil, making sure the foil does not come into contact with the food. Simmer for 35–40 minutes or until the lamb is tender.

4 Put the chana dhal or split peas into a large pan with the remaining measured water and a good pinch of salt and boil for 12–15 minutes, or until the water has almost evaporated and the lentils or peas are soft enough to be mashed. If they are too thick, add up to 150ml/¼ pint/⅔ cup water.

5 When the lamb is tender, remove the lid or foil and stir-fry the mixture using a wooden spoon, until some free oil begins to appear on the sides of the pan.

6 Add the cooked lentils to the lamb and mix together well. Stir in the tomatoes, chillies and chopped fresh coriander and serve.

COOK'S TIP
Boned and cubed chicken can be used in place of the lamb. At step 3, reduce the amount of water to about 300ml/½ pint/1¼ cups and cook uncovered, stirring occasionally, for 10–15 minutes, or until the water has evaporated and the chicken is cooked through.

MUGHLAI-STYLE LEG of LAMB

In India, there are different names for this style of cooking a leg of lamb, two of which are shahi raan *and* peshawari raan. *Roasting a whole leg of lamb was first popularized by the Mongolian warrior Genghis Khan (1162–1227) and is known as Chengezi Raan.*

SERVES 4–6

4 large onions, chopped
4 garlic cloves
5cm/2in piece fresh root ginger,
    chopped
45ml/3 tbsp ground almonds
10ml/2 tsp ground cumin
10ml/2 tsp ground coriander
10ml/2 tsp ground turmeric
10ml/2 tsp garam masala
4–6 fresh green chillies
juice of 1 lemon
300ml/½ pint/1¼ cups natural (plain)
    yogurt, beaten
1.8kg/4lb leg of lamb
8–10 cloves
salt
15ml/1 tbsp blanched almond flakes,
    to garnish
4 firm tomatoes, halved and grilled
    (broiled), to serve

1 Place the first ten ingredients in a food processor or blender, with salt to taste, and process to a smooth paste. Gradually add the yogurt and blend. Grease a large, deep roasting pan and preheat the oven to 190°C/375°F/Gas 5.

2 Remove most of the fat and skin from the lamb. Using a sharp knife, make deep pockets above the bone at each side of the thick end. Make deep diagonal gashes on both sides of the lamb.

COOK'S TIP
If time permits, allow the joint to stand at room temperature for a couple of hours before putting it in the oven.

3 Push the cloves firmly into the meat, spaced evenly on all sides.

4 Push some of the spice mixture into the pockets and gashes and spread the remainder evenly all over the meat. Place the meat on the roasting pan and loosely cover the whole pan with foil. Roast for 2–2½ hours, or until the meat is cooked, removing the foil for the last 10 minutes of cooking time.

5 Remove from the oven and allow to rest for about 10 minutes before carving. Garnish the joint with almond flakes, and serve with grilled tomatoes.

SHAMMI KABAB

Kababs came to India from the Middle East, where the word is spelt kebab and refers to a skewered meat. There is a delectable range of kababs in Indian cuisine, most of which can be served either as appetizers or side dishes with an accompanying raita or chutney.

SERVES 5–6

2 onions, finely chopped
250g/9oz lean lamb, boned and cubed
50g/2oz chana dhal or yellow split peas
5ml/1 tsp cumin seeds
5ml/1 tsp garam masala
4–6 fresh green chillies
5cm/2in piece fresh root ginger, grated
175ml/6fl oz/¾ cup water
a few fresh coriander (cilantro) and mint
    leaves, chopped, plus extra coriander
    (cilantro) sprigs to garnish
juice of 1 lemon
15ml/1 tbsp gram flour (besan)
2 eggs, beaten
vegetable oil, for shallow frying
salt

1 Put the first seven ingredients and the water into a large pan with salt, and bring to the boil. Simmer, covered, until the meat and dhal are cooked. Remove the lid and continue to cook for a few more minutes, to reduce the excess liquid. Set aside to cool.

2 Transfer the cooled meat and dhal mixture to a food processor or blender and process to a rough paste.

3 Put the paste into a large mixing bowl and add the chopped coriander and mint leaves, lemon juice and gram flour. Knead well with your hands to make sure the ingredients are evenly distributed through the mixture.

4 Divide the mixture into 10–12 even-size portions and use your hands to roll each into a ball, then flatten slightly. Chill for 1 hour. Dip the kabab in the beaten egg and shallow fry each side until golden brown. Pat dry on kitchen paper and serve hot.

ROGAN JOSH

This is one of the most popular lamb dishes to have originated in Kashmir. Traditionally, fatty meat on the bone is slow cooked until most of the fat is separated from the meat. The fat that escapes from the meat in this way is known as rogan and josh refers to the rich red colour. The Kashmiris achieve this colour by using a combination of mild and bright Kashmiri chillies and the juice extracted from a brightly coloured local flower.

SERVES 4–6

45ml/3 tbsp lemon juice
250ml/8fl oz/1 cup natural (plain) yogurt
5ml/1 tsp salt
2 garlic cloves, crushed
2.5cm/1in piece fresh root ginger, finely grated
900g/2lb lean lamb fillet, cubed
60ml/4 tbsp vegetable oil
2.5ml/½ tsp cumin seeds
2 bay leaves
4 green cardamom pods
1 onion, finely chopped
10ml/2 tsp ground coriander
10ml/2 tsp ground cumin
5ml/1 tsp chilli powder
400g/14oz can chopped tomatoes
30ml/2 tbsp tomato purée (paste)
150ml/¼ pint/⅔ cup water
toasted cumin seeds and bay leaves, to garnish
plain boiled rice, to serve

1 In a large bowl, mix together the lemon juice, yogurt, salt, one crushed garlic clove and the ginger. Add the lamb and marinate in the refrigerator overnight.

2 Heat the oil in a wok, karahi or large pan and fry the cumin seeds for 2 minutes until they splutter. Add the bay leaves and cardamom pods and fry for 2 minutes.

3 Add the onion and remaining garlic and fry for 5 minutes. Add the coriander, cumin and chilli powder. Fry for 2 minutes.

4 Add the marinated lamb to the pan and cook for a further 5 minutes, stirring occasionally to prevent the mixture from sticking to the base of the pan.

5 Add the tomatoes, tomato purée and water. Cover and simmer for 1–1½ hours. Garnish with toasted cumin seeds and bay leaves, and serve.

MINCED LAMB with PEAS

This dish, known as kheema mattar, is a favourite all over India, although it originated in the north. Generally, in India minced mutton is used, as lamb is not very easy to obtain. Minced turkey, pork or chicken would all work equally well.

SERVES 4

45ml/3 tbsp vegetable oil
1 onion, finely chopped
2 garlic cloves, crushed
2.5cm/1in piece fresh root ginger, grated
2 fresh green chillies, finely chopped
675g/1½lb minced (ground) lamb
5ml/1 tsp ground cumin
5ml/1 tsp ground coriander
5ml/1 tsp chilli powder
5ml/1 tsp salt
175g/6oz/1½ cups frozen peas, thawed
30ml/2 tbsp lemon juice
naan and natural (plain) yogurt, to serve

3 Stir in the cumin, coriander, chilli powder and salt with 300ml/½ pint/ 1¼ cups water. Cover the pan and simmer for about 25 minutes.

4 Add the peas and lemon juice. Cook for 10 minutes, uncovered. Garnish with fresh coriander and chilli powder and serve with warm naan and natural yogurt.

1 Heat the oil and fry the onion for about 5 minutes over a medium heat until browned. Add the garlic, ginger and chillies and fry for 2–3 minutes.

2 Add the minced lamb and stir-fry briskly for 5 minutes over a high heat.

COOK'S TIP
To reduce the fat content, dry-fry the lamb in a non-stick frying pan until the natural fat is released. Drain the fat and use the lamb as directed in the recipe.

LAMB with APRICOTS

This recipe comes from the wonderful fruit-laden valley of Kashmir. The cuisine of Kashmir is renowned for the imaginative use of all the exotic fruits and nuts that grow abundantly in that state. Serve with an apricot chutney to complement the fruit in the recipe.

2 Heat the oil in a wok, karahi or large pan and fry the cinnamon stick and cardamoms for 2 minutes. Add the onion and fry for 6–8 minutes until soft.

3 Add the curry paste and fry for about 2 minutes. Stir in the cumin, coriander and salt and fry for 2–3 minutes.

4 Add the cubed lamb, dried apricots and the lamb stock to the pan. Cover with the lid and cook over a medium heat for 1–1½ hours.

5 Transfer to a serving dish and garnish with the fresh coriander. Classic Pulao and Apricot Chutney would make good accompaniments to this dish.

SERVES 4–6

900g/2lb stewing lamb
30ml/2 tbsp vegetable oil
2.5cm/1in piece cinnamon stick
4 green cardamom pods
1 onion, chopped
15ml/1 tbsp curry paste
5ml/1 tsp ground cumin
5ml/1 tsp ground coriander
1.5ml/¼ tsp salt
175g/6oz/¾ cup ready-to-eat dried apricots
350ml/12fl oz/1½ cups lamb stock
fresh coriander (cilantro), to garnish

1 Cut away and discard any visible fat from the lamb, then cut the meat into 2.5cm/1in cubes.

LAMB KOFTA CURRY

Koftas, or meatballs, reveal a Middle Eastern influence on Indian cuisine. The Middle Eastern technique for making the meatballs is still used, combined with the skilful blending of Indian spices. Koftas make an inexpensive but delicious main course.

SERVES 4

675g/1½lb minced (ground) lamb
1 fresh green chilli, roughly chopped
1 garlic clove, chopped
2.5cm/1in piece fresh root ginger, chopped
1.5ml/¼ tsp garam masala
1.5ml/¼ tsp salt
45ml/3 tbsp chopped fresh coriander
   (cilantro)

For the sauce
30ml/2 tbsp vegetable oil
2.5ml/½ tsp cumin seeds
1 onion, chopped
1 garlic clove, chopped
2.5cm/1in piece fresh root ginger,
   grated
5ml/1 tsp ground cumin
5ml/1 tsp ground coriander
2.5ml/½ tsp salt
2.5ml/½ tsp chilli powder
15ml/1 tbsp tomato purée (paste)
400g/14oz can chopped tomatoes
fresh coriander (cilantro) sprigs,
   to garnish
coriander (cilantro) rice, to serve

1 To make the meatballs, put the lamb, chilli, garlic, ginger, garam masala, salt and coriander into a food processor and process until the mixture binds together.

2 Shape the mixture into 16 balls, using your hands. Cover with clear film (plastic wrap) and chill for 10 minutes.

COOK'S TIP
You can make the meatballs the day before. Store them in the refrigerator until needed.

3 To make the sauce, heat the oil and fry the cumin seeds until they splutter. Add the onion, garlic and ginger and fry for 5 minutes. Stir in the remaining sauce ingredients and simmer for 5 minutes.

4 Add the meatballs. Bring to the boil, cover and simmer for 25–30 minutes, or until the meatballs are cooked through. Garnish with sprigs of fresh coriander and serve with coriander rice.

KARAHI LAMB

Lamb dishes are a speciality in the state of Kashmir, the only region of India where the climate is ideal for rearing lamb. Karahi lamb is widely eaten, and in this version the sautéed dried apricots flavoured with cinnamon and cardamom add an irresistible touch.

SERVES 4

15ml/1 tbsp tomato purée (paste)
175ml/6fl oz/¾ cup natural (plain) yogurt
5ml/1 tsp garam masala
1.5ml/¼ tsp cumin seeds
5ml/1 tsp salt
5ml/1 tsp crushed garlic
5ml/1 tsp grated fresh root ginger
5ml/1 tsp chilli powder
450g/1lb lean spring lamb, cut into strips
30ml/2 tbsp vegetable oil
2 onions, finely sliced
25g/1oz ghee, butter or margarine
2.5cm/1in piece cinnamon stick
2 green cardamom pods
5 dried apricots, quartered
15ml/1 tbsp chopped fresh coriander
   (cilantro)

1 In a bowl, blend the tomato purée, yogurt, garam masala, cumin seeds, salt, garlic, ginger and chilli powder. Add the lamb and leave to marinate for 1 hour.

2 Heat 10ml/2 tsp of the oil in a wok, karahi or large pan and fry the onions until crisp and golden brown.

3 Remove the onions using a slotted spoon, allow them to cool and then grind them down by processing briefly in a food processor or blender, or with a pestle in a mortar. Reheat the oil and return the onions to the pan.

4 Add the lamb and stir-fry for about 2 minutes. Cover the pan, lower the heat and cook, stirring occasionally, for 15 minutes, or until the meat is cooked through. If required, add up to 150ml/¼ pint/⅔ cup water during the cooking. Remove from the heat and set aside.

5 Heat the ghee, butter or margarine with the remaining oil and add the cinnamon stick and cardamoms. Stir in the apricots and cook over a low heat for 2 minutes. Pour this sauce over the lamb.

6 Garnish with the chopped coriander leaves and serve immediately.

COOK'S TIP
If you want this curry to be slightly hotter, increase the garam masala and chilli powder to 7.5ml/1½ tsp each.

STIR-FRIED CHILLI-GARLIC PRAWNS

*Prawns have a particular affinity with garlic. To enhance the flavour of the garlic,
fry it very gently without letting it brown completely. The spice-coated prawns make
a mouthwatering appetizer or light lunch, when served with a salad, or they can be
transformed into a main meal with the addition of warm naan bread.*

SERVES 4

15ml/1 tbsp vegetable oil
3 garlic cloves, roughly halved
3 tomatoes, chopped
2.5ml/½ tsp salt
5ml/1 tsp crushed dried red chillies
5ml/1 tsp lemon juice
Mango Chutney, to taste
1 fresh green chilli, chopped
16–20 peeled, cooked king prawns
    (jumbo shrimp)
fresh coriander (cilantro) sprigs and
    chopped spring onions (scallions),
    to garnish

1 In a wok, karahi or large pan, heat the
vegetable oil over a low heat and fry the
garlic halves gently until they are tinged
with golden brown.

2 Add the chopped tomatoes, salt,
crushed red chillies, lemon juice, Mango
Chutney and the chopped fresh chilli.
Stir the ingredients well.

3 Add the prawns to the pan, then raise
the heat and stir-fry briskly, mixing the
prawns with the other ingredients until
they are thoroughly heated through.

4 Transfer the prawns in the sauce to a
warm serving dish and garnish with fresh
coriander sprigs and chopped spring
onions. Serve immediately.

GRILLED KING PRAWNS with STIR-FRIED SPICES

Traditionally, king prawns are marinated and then grilled in the tandoor to produce the delectable tandoori king prawns. It is possible to achieve similar results by grilling the prawns under a very hot electric or gas grill as in this recipe.

SERVES 4

45ml/3 tbsp natural (plain) yogurt
5ml/1 tsp paprika
5ml/1 tsp grated fresh root ginger
16–20 peeled, cooked king prawns (jumbo shrimp), thawed if frozen
15ml/1 tbsp vegetable oil
3 onions, sliced
2.5ml/½ tsp fennel seeds, crushed
2.5cm/1in piece cinnamon stick
5ml/1 tsp crushed garlic
5ml/1 tsp chilli powder
1 yellow (bell) pepper, seeded and roughly chopped
1 red (bell) pepper, seeded and roughly chopped
salt
15ml/1 tbsp fresh coriander (cilantro) leaves, to garnish

1 Blend together the yogurt, paprika, ginger and add salt to taste. Add to the prawns and leave in a cool place to marinate for 30–45 minutes.

2 Meanwhile, heat the oil in a wok, karahi or large pan and fry the sliced onions with the fennel seeds and the cinnamon stick over a medium heat until the onions soften and turn golden.

3 Lower the heat and stir in the crushed garlic and chilli powder.

4 Add the chopped yellow and red peppers to the pan and stir-fry gently for 3–5 minutes.

5 Remove the pan from the heat and transfer the onion and spice mixture to a warm serving dish, discarding the cinnamon stick. Set the dish aside.

COOK'S TIP
It is important not to overcook the prawns, they only need heating through.

6 Preheat the grill (broiler) to medium. Put the marinated prawns in a grill pan or flameproof dish and place under the grill to darken their tops and achieve a chargrilled effect. Add the prawns to the onion and spice mixture, and garnish with fresh coriander. Serve with plain rice and Creamy Black Lentils, if you like.

CORN on the COB in RICH ONION SAUCE

Corn is grown extensively in the Punjab region, where it is used in many delicacies. Corn bread, makki ki roti, *along with spiced mustard greens,* sarson ka saag, *is a combination that is hard to beat and is what the Punjabis thrive on. Here, corn is cooked in a thick rich onion sauce, in another classic Punjabi dish. It is excellent served with naan bread.*

SERVES 4–6

4 corn cobs, thawed if frozen
vegetable oil, for frying
1 large onion, finely chopped
2 cloves garlic, crushed
5cm/2in piece fresh root ginger, crushed
2.5ml/½ tsp ground turmeric
2.5ml/½ tsp onion seeds
2.5ml/½ tsp cumin seeds
2.5ml/½ tsp five-spice powder
6–8 curry leaves
2.5ml/½ tsp granulated sugar
200ml/7fl oz/scant 1 cup natural (plain) yogurt
chilli powder, to taste

1 Cut each corn cob in half, using a heavy knife or cleaver to make clean cuts. Heat the oil in a wok, karahi or large pan and fry the corn until golden brown. Remove the corn and set aside.

2 Remove any excess oil, leaving 30ml/ 2 tbsp in the wok. Grind the onion, garlic and ginger to a paste using a pestle and mortar or in a food processor. Transfer the paste to a bowl and mix in the spices, chilli powder, curry leaves and sugar.

3 Heat the oil gently and fry the onion paste mixture for 8–10 minutes until all the spices have blended well and the oil separates from the sauce.

4 Cool the mixture and fold in the yogurt. Mix to a smooth sauce. Add the corn and mix well, so that all the pieces are covered with the sauce. Reheat gently for about 10 minutes. Serve hot.

STIR-FRIED INDIAN CHEESE with MUSHROOMS and PEAS

Indian cheese, known as paneer, *is a very versatile ingredient. It is used in both sweet and savoury dishes. Indian housewives generally make this cheese at home, although in recent years it has become available commercially. It is a useful source of protein for the the people in the north who are vegetarian.*

SERVES 4–6

90ml/6 tbsp ghee or vegetable oil
225g/8oz paneer, cubed
1 onion, finely chopped
a few fresh mint leaves, chopped, plus
    extra sprigs to garnish
50g/2oz chopped fresh coriander (cilantro)
3 fresh green chillies, chopped
3 garlic cloves
2.5cm/1in piece fresh root ginger, sliced
5ml/1 tsp ground turmeric
5ml/1 tsp chilli powder (optional)
5ml/1 tsp garam masala
225g/8oz/3 cups tiny button (white)
    mushrooms, washed
225g/8oz/2 cups frozen peas, thawed
175ml/6fl oz/¾ cup natural (plain) yogurt,
    mixed with 5ml/1 tsp cornflour
    (cornstarch)
salt

1 Heat the ghee or oil in a wok, karahi or large pan, and fry the paneer cubes until they are golden brown on all sides. Remove, drain on kitchen paper, and keep to one side.

2 Grind the onion, mint, coriander, chillies, garlic and ginger with a pestle and mortar or in a food processor to a fairly smooth paste.

3 Remove to a bowl and mix in the turmeric, chilli powder, if using, and garam masala, and season with salt to taste.

4 Remove excess ghee or oil from the pan, leaving about 15ml/1 tbsp. Heat and fry the paste over a medium heat for 8–10 minutes, or until the raw onion smell disappears and the oil separates.

5 Add the mushrooms, thawed peas and paneer, and mix well. Cool the mixture slightly and gradually fold in the yogurt.

6 Simmer for about 10 minutes, until the vegetables are tender and the flavours well mixed. Remove to a serving dish, garnish with sprigs of fresh mint and serve immediately.

COOK'S TIP

If paneer is not available, you can use grilled goat's cheese instead. Add it just before the garnish.

DRY-SPICED POTATOES with CAULIFLOWER

This dish, known as aloo gobi *in most Indian restaurants, has remained one of the most popular over the years. It is also a healthy dish, as potatoes are 90 per cent fat free and both potatoes and cauliflower are good sources of vitamin C.*

2 Heat the oil in a wok, karahi or large pan over a medium heat and fry the cumin seeds for 2 minutes until they begin to splutter. Add the fresh green chilli and fry for a further 1 minute.

3 Add the cauliflower florets to the pan and fry, stirring, for 5 minutes.

4 Add the potatoes, the spices and salt and cook for a further 7–10 minutes, or until both vegetables are tender. Garnish with chopped coriander and serve with Tomato and Onion Salad and a pickle.

SERVES 4

450g/1lb potatoes
30ml/2 tbsp vegetable oil
5ml/1 tsp cumin seeds
1 fresh green chilli, finely chopped
450g/1lb cauliflower, broken into florets
5ml/1 tsp ground coriander
5ml/1 tsp ground cumin
1.5ml/¼ tsp chilli powder
2.5ml/½ tsp ground turmeric
2.5ml/½ tsp salt
chopped fresh coriander (cilantro),
   to garnish
Tomato and Onion Salad and a pickle of
   your choice, to serve

1 Cut the peeled and washed potatoes into 2.5cm/1in cubes, then par-boil them in a large pan of boiling water for about 10 minutes. Drain the potatoes well and set them aside.

VARIATION
Use broccoli instead of some or all of the cauliflower, if you prefer.

KARAHI POTATOES with WHOLE SPICES

All spices work like magic with potatoes. Even just a light touch can bring about a complete transformation. For this recipe choose floury potatoes, as they will absorb the spice flavours better than the waxy variety.

SERVES 4

45ml/3 tbsp vegetable oil
2.5ml/½ tsp white cumin seeds
3 curry leaves
5ml/1 tsp crushed dried red chillies
2.5ml/½ tsp mixed onion, mustard
 and fenugreek seeds
2.5ml/½ tsp fennel seeds
3 garlic cloves, roughly chopped
2.5ml/½ tsp grated fresh root ginger
2 onions, sliced
6 new potatoes, cut into 5mm/¼in slices
15ml/1 tbsp chopped fresh coriander
 (cilantro)
1 fresh red chilli, seeded and sliced
1 fresh green chilli, seeded and sliced

1 Heat the oil in a wok, karahi or large pan. Lower the heat slightly and add the cumin seeds, curry leaves, dried chillies, mixed onion, mustard and fenugreek seeds, fennel seeds, chopped garlic and grated ginger.

2 Fry for about 1 minute, then add the sliced onions and fry gently for a further 5 minutes, or until the onions are golden brown. Add the sliced potatoes, fresh coriander and red and green chillies. Mix together well. Cover the pan tightly with a lid or foil, making sure the foil does not touch the food. Cook over a very low heat for about 7 minutes, or until the potatoes are tender.

3 Remove the lid or foil from the pan and serve the potatoes hot with parathas and any lentil dish for a vegetarian meal. Serve Shammi Kabab, Tandoori Chicken or Chicken Tikka instead of the lentils for meat eaters.

MUSHROOM CURRY

In India, mushrooms traditionally grow only in the northern state of Kashmir. However, Indians have acquired the taste for them due to frequent travels abroad, and they are now being cultivated in other northern areas where the climate is suitable.

2 Add the onion and fry for 5 minutes or until golden. Stir in the ground cumin, coriander and garam masala and fry for a further 2 minutes.

3 Add the chilli, garlic and ginger and fry for 2–3 minutes, stirring constantly. Add the tomatoes and salt. Bring to the boil and simmer for 5 minutes.

SERVES 4

30ml/2 tbsp vegetable oil
2.5ml/½ tsp cumin seeds
1.5ml/¼ tsp black peppercorns
4 green cardamom pods
1.5ml/¼ tsp ground turmeric
1 onion, finely chopped
5ml/1 tsp ground cumin
5ml/1 tsp ground coriander
2.5ml/½ tsp garam masala
1 fresh green chilli, finely chopped
2 garlic cloves, crushed
2.5cm/1in piece fresh root ginger, grated
400g/4oz can chopped tomatoes
1.5ml/¼ tsp salt
450g/1lb/6 cups button (white) mushrooms
chopped fresh coriander (cilantro),
    to garnish

1 Heat the vegetable oil in a wok, karahi or large pan and fry the cumin seeds, black peppercorns, cardamom pods and turmeric for 2–3 minutes.

COOK'S TIP
For authentic Kashmiri style, use ground or crushed fennel in place of the cumin.

4 Halve the mushrooms, then add them to the pan. Cover and simmer over a low heat for 10 minutes. Transfer to a warm serving platter and garnish with chopped coriander. Serve with an Indian bread, such as naan, parathas or chapatis, and any dry meat or poultry dish, such as Shammi Kabab or Tandoori Chicken.

COURGETTES in SPICED TOMATO SAUCE

In India, tender marrow would be used for this recipe as courgettes are not grown there. Do try this recipe with a young marrow in the summer. It will also work well with winter squashes, such as butternut and acorn.

SERVES 4

675g/1½lb courgettes (zucchini)
45ml/3 tbsp vegetable oil
2.5ml/½ tsp cumin seeds
2.5ml/½ tsp mustard seeds
1 onion, thinly sliced
2 garlic cloves, crushed
1.5ml/¼ tsp ground turmeric
1.5ml/¼ tsp chilli powder
5ml/1 tsp ground coriander
5ml/1 tsp ground cumin
2.5ml/½ tsp salt
15ml/1 tbsp tomato purée (paste)
400g/14oz can chopped tomatoes
150ml/¼ pint/⅔ cup water
15ml/1 tbsp chopped fresh coriander
   (cilantro)
5ml/1 tsp garam masala

4 Add the ground turmeric, chilli powder, coriander, cumin and salt and fry for about 2–3 minutes.

5 Add the sliced courgettes, and cook for 5 minutes. Add the tomato purée and chopped tomatoes to the pan.

6 Add the water, then cover the pan and simmer for 10 minutes until the sauce thickens. Stir in the fresh coriander and garam masala, then cook for about 5 minutes, or until the courgettes are tender. Serve as an accompaniment to any meat, poultry or fish dish.

1 Trim the ends from the courgettes then cut them into 1cm/½in thick slices.

2 Heat the oil in a wok, karahi or large pan. Fry the cumin and mustard seeds for 2 minutes until they begin to splutter.

3 Add the onion and garlic and fry for about 5–6 minutes.

CUMIN-SCENTED VEGETABLES with TOASTED ALMONDS

Cabbage is a traditional vegetable in India, although neither baby corn cobs nor mangetouts are used in Indian cooking. Nonetheless, combining new and traditional ideas can create exciting and original dishes, as this recipe shows.

SERVES 4

15ml/1 tbsp vegetable oil
50g/2oz/4 tbsp butter
2.5ml/½ tsp crushed coriander seeds
2.5ml/½ tsp white cumin seeds
6 dried red chillies
1 small savoy cabbage, shredded
12 mangetouts (snow peas)
3 fresh red chillies, seeded and sliced
12 baby corn cobs, halved
salt
25g/1oz/¼ cup flaked (sliced) almonds, toasted and 15ml/1 tbsp chopped fresh coriander (cilantro), to garnish

1 Heat the oil and butter in a wok, karahi or large pan and add the crushed coriander seeds, white cumin seeds and dried red chillies.

2 Add the shredded cabbage and mangetouts to the spices in the pan and stir-fry briskly for about 5 minutes, until the cabbage starts to turn crisp.

3 Add the fresh red chillies, and baby corn cobs to the pan and season with salt to taste. Stir-fry for 3 minutes more.

4 Garnish with the toasted almonds and fresh coriander, and serve hot. This dish would go well with any meat curry and with Classic Pulao.

COOK'S TIP
Julienne strips of other vegetables will make this dish visually more appealing, and will add superb taste at the same time. Try julienne carrots and leeks instead of mangetouts and baby corn. Add the cabbage and carrots together, and add the leeks in step 3.

ROASTED AUBERGINES with SPRING ONIONS

This classic dish, made of roasted and mashed aubergines cooked with spring onions, is known as bharta *in the Punjab region. The term* bharta *means to mash. Traditionally, the aubergine is roasted over charcoal, but a hot electric or gas oven will produce similar results, although the smoky flavour will be missing.*

SERVES 4

2 large aubergines (eggplant)
45ml/3 tbsp vegetable oil
2.5ml/½ tsp black mustard seeds
1 bunch spring onions (scallions),
 finely chopped
115g/4oz/1½ cups button (white)
 mushrooms, halved
2 garlic cloves, crushed
1 fresh red chilli, finely chopped
2.5ml/½ tsp chilli powder
5ml/1 tsp ground cumin
5ml/1 tsp ground coriander
1.5ml/¼ tsp ground turmeric
5ml/1 tsp salt
400g/14oz can chopped tomatoes
15ml/1 tbsp chopped fresh coriander
 (cilantro), plus a few extra sprigs
 to garnish

1 Preheat the oven to 200°C/400°F/ Gas 6. Brush both of the aubergines with 15ml/1 tbsp of oil and prick with a fork. Bake for 30–35 minutes until soft.

2 Meanwhile, heat the remaining oil and fry the black mustard seeds for about 2 minutes until they splutter. Add the onions, mushrooms, garlic and chilli, and fry for 5 minutes more. Stir in the chilli powder, cumin, coriander, turmeric and salt and fry for 3–4 minutes. Add the tomatoes and simmer for 5 minutes.

COOK'S TIP

Roast the aubergines (eggplant) over a barbecue for an authentic smoky flavour.

3 Cut the aubergines in half lengthwise and scoop out the soft flesh into a large mixing bowl. Mash the flesh to a course texture, using a fork.

4 Add the aubergines to the pan with the coriander. Bring to the boil and simmer for 5 minutes until the sauce thickens. Serve garnished with coriander.

KIDNEY BEAN CURRY

This dish, known as rajma *in Punjabi, is a fine example of the area's hearty, robust cuisine. It is widely eaten dish all over the state, and is even sold by street vendors. Plain boiled rice makes the perfect accompaniment for this dish.*

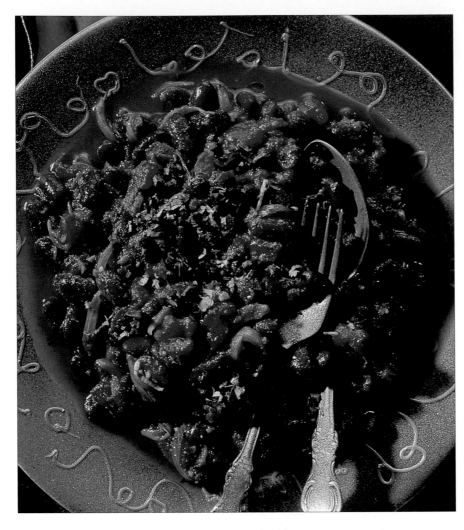

SERVES 4

225g/8oz/1¼ cups dried red kidney beans
30ml/2 tbsp vegetable oil
2.5ml/½ tsp cumin seeds
1 onion, thinly sliced
1 fresh green chilli, finely chopped
2 garlic cloves, crushed
2.5cm/1in piece fresh root ginger, grated
30ml/2 tbsp curry paste
5ml/1 tsp ground cumin
5ml/1 tsp ground coriander
2.5ml/½ tsp chilli powder
2.5ml/½ tsp salt
400g/14oz can chopped tomatoes
30ml/2 tbsp chopped fresh
    coriander (cilantro)

1 Place the kidney beans in a large bowl of cold water and then leave them to soak overnight.

2 Drain the beans and place in a large pan with double the volume of water. Boil vigorously for 10 minutes. Drain, rinse and return the beans to the pan. Add double the volume of water and bring to the boil. Reduce the heat, then cover and cook for 1–1½ hours, or until the beans are soft. This process is essential in order to remove the toxins that are present in dried kidney beans.

3 Meanwhile, heat the oil in a wok, karahi or large pan and fry the cumin seeds for 2 minutes until they begin to splutter. Add the onion, chilli, garlic and ginger and fry for 5 minutes. Stir in the curry paste, cumin, coriander, chilli powder and salt, and cook for 5 minutes.

4 Add the tomatoes and simmer for 5 minutes. Add the beans and fresh coriander, reserving a little for the garnish. Cover and cook for 15 minutes adding a little water if necessary. Serve garnished with the reserved coriander.

COOK'S TIP
Drained and well-rinsed canned beans work very well as an alternative.

CREAMY BLACK LENTILS

Black lentils or urad dhal *are available whole, split, and skinned and split. Generally, both split, and skinned and split versions are used in west and south Indian cooking, whereas whole black lentils are a typical ingredient in the north.*

SERVES 4–6

175g/6oz/¾ cup black lentils, soaked
50g/2oz/¼ cup red split lentils
120ml/4fl oz/½ cup double (heavy) cream
120ml/4fl oz/½ cup natural (plain) yogurt
5ml/1 tsp cornflour (cornstarch)
45ml/3 tbsp ghee or vegetable oil
1 onion, finely chopped
5cm/2in piece fresh root ginger, crushed
4 fresh green chillies, chopped
1 tomato, chopped
2.5ml/½ tsp chilli powder
2.5ml/½ tsp ground turmeric
2.5ml/½ tsp ground cumin
2 garlic cloves, sliced
salt
coriander (cilantro) sprigs and sliced
    red chilli, to garnish

3 Heat 15ml/1 tbsp of the ghee or oil in a wok, karahi or large pan, and fry the onion, ginger, two green chillies and the tomato until the onion is soft. Add the ground spices and salt and fry for a further 2 minutes. Stir into the lentil mixture and mix well. Reheat, transfer to a heatproof serving dish and keep warm.

4 Heat the remaining ghee or oil in a frying pan over a low heat and fry the garlic slices and remaining chillies until the garlic slices are golden brown. Pour over the lentils and fold the garlic and chilli into the lentils just before serving. Place extra cream on the table for the diners to add more if they wish.

1 Drain the black lentils and place in a large pan with the red lentils. Cover with water and bring to the boil. Reduce the heat, cover the pan and simmer until tender. Mash with a spoon, and cool.

2 In a bowl, mix together the cream, yogurt and cornflour, and stir into the lentils in the pan.

EAST INDIA

The state of Bengal has developed a strong culinary identity, which makes use of local produce such as mustard, coconut, vegetables, lentils and rice. Fish from the Bay of Bengal is eaten throughout eastern India, and in areas close to the sea, fish is eaten daily, in place of meat.

CHICKEN JHALFRAZI

Jhalfrazi was created by Indian chefs during the British Raj. Leftover cold meat, generally from the Sunday roast, was stir-fried with spices. The dish originated in Calcutta, where the East India Company was established as an important trading post by the British.

SERVES 4

675g/1½lb chicken breast fillets, skinned
30ml/2 tbsp vegetable oil
5ml/1 tsp cumin seeds
1 onion, finely chopped
1 green (bell) pepper, finely chopped
1 red (bell) pepper, finely chopped
1 garlic clove, crushed
2cm/¾in piece fresh root ginger, chopped
15ml/1 tbsp curry paste
1.5ml/¼ tsp chilli powder
5ml/1 tsp ground coriander
5ml/1 tsp ground cumin
2.5ml/½ tsp salt
400g/14oz can chopped tomatoes
30ml/2 tbsp chopped fresh coriander
    (cilantro)
fresh coriander (cilantro) sprig, to garnish
plain boiled rice or naan bread, to serve

3 Add the curry paste to the other ingredients in the pan and stir-fry for about 2 minutes. Stir in the chilli powder, ground coriander, cumin and salt, and add 15ml/1 tbsp water. Stir-fry for a further 2 minutes.

4 Add the chicken and stir-fry for about 5 minutes. Add the tomatoes and fresh coriander. Cook, covered, for about 15 minutes until the chicken is tender. Garnish with a sprig of fresh coriander. Serve with plain boiled rice or naan.

1 Remove any visible fat and cut the chicken into 2.5cm/1in cubes.

2 Heat the oil in a wok, karahi or large pan, and fry the cumin seeds for 30–40 seconds until they begin to splutter. Add the onion, peppers, garlic and ginger and fry for 6–8 minutes.

CUMIN-SCENTED CHICKEN

Cumin is a wonderful spice that is full of pungency, but without any harshness. Its rather warm and assertive nature gives this dish a distinctive flavour and aroma. Cumin is also known to have curative properties.

SERVES 4

45ml/3 tbsp cumin seeds
45ml/3 tbsp vegetable oil
2.5ml/½ tsp black peppercorns
4 green cardamom pods
2 fresh green chillies, finely chopped
2 garlic cloves, crushed
2.5cm/1in piece fresh root ginger, grated
5ml/1 tsp ground coriander
10ml/2 tsp ground cumin
2.5ml/½ tsp salt
8 chicken pieces, such as thighs and
    drumsticks, skinned
5ml/1 tsp garam masala
Cucumber Raita, garnished with fresh
    coriander (cilantro) and chilli powder,
    to serve (optional)

1 Preheat a wok or round-based frying pan over a medium heat and dry-roast 15ml/1 tbsp of the cumin seeds for 1–2 minutes until they release their aroma. Set aside.

2 Heat the oil in a wok or large pan and fry the remaining cumin seeds, black peppercorns and cardamoms for about 2 minutes.

3 Add the green chillies, garlic and grated fresh root ginger to the spices in the pan and fry for 2 minutes.

4 Add the ground coriander and cumin to the pan with the salt, and cook over a medium heat, stirring, for a further 1–2 minutes.

5 Add the chicken pieces, stir and mix thoroughly with the spices. Cover and allow to simmer for 20–25 minutes.

6 Add the garam masala and reserved dry-roasted cumin seeds, and cook for a further 5 minutes. Serve with Cucumber Raita, if you like.

CHICKEN in COCONUT MILK

In Bengal, this dish is known as murgi malai, *and in the Bengali language, the word* murgi *means chicken and* malai *is cream, either dairy or coconut. Coconut is a favourite ingredient of the region, and it grows in adundant supply in Bengal, Orissa and Assam.*

2 Add the coconut milk, fromage frais or ricotta cheese, ground coriander, chilli powder, garlic, ginger and salt to the bowl. Mix together well.

3 Heat the vegetable oil in the pan, and add the chicken cubes, cardamom pods and bay leaf. Stir-fry for about 2 minutes to seal the chicken.

SERVES 4

15ml/1 tbsp ground almonds
15ml/1 tbsp desiccated (dry, unsweetened, shredded) coconut
85ml/3fl oz/⅔ cup coconut milk
175g/6oz/⅔ cup fromage frais or ricotta cheese
7.5ml/1½ tsp ground coriander
5ml/1 tsp chilli powder
5ml/1 tsp crushed garlic
7.5ml/1½ tsp grated fresh root ginger
5ml/1 tsp salt
30ml/2 tbsp vegetable oil
450g/1lb chicken breast fillets, skinned and cubed
3 green cardamom pods
1 bay leaf
1 dried red chilli, crushed
30ml/2 tbsp chopped fresh coriander (cilantro)

1 Dry-roast the almonds and coconut in a wok, karahi or large pan, until they turn a shade darker. Transfer the mixture to a large glass bowl.

COOK'S TIP
Fromage frais and ricotta cheese are used here in order to reduce the fat content. For a more authentic taste and aroma, use extra coconut milk.

4 Pour in the coconut mixture and stir well. Lower the heat, add the chilli and coriander, then cover and cook for 10–12 minutes, stirring occasionally to prevent the contents from sticking to the pan. Uncover the pan, then stir and cook for 2 minutes more. Classic Pulao would make a good accompaniment.

FISH JHALFRAZI

In Bengal, fish curry and rice are eaten together on a daily basis. This is a rather unusual dish, using canned tuna cooked in the style of jhalfrazi, and is ideal for lunch or supper. Served with boiled basmati rice and tarka dhal, it will also make a satisfying family meal.

SERVES 4

1 onion
1 red (bell) pepper
1 green (bell) pepper
45ml/3 tbsp vegetable oil
1.5ml/¼ tsp cumin seeds
2.5ml/½ tsp ground cumin
2.5ml/½ tsp ground coriander
2.5ml/½ tsp chilli powder
1.5ml/¼ tsp salt
2 garlic cloves, crushed
400g/14oz can tuna, drained
1 fresh green chilli, finely chopped
2.5cm/1in piece fresh root ginger, grated
1.5ml/¼ tsp garam masala
5ml/1 tsp lemon juice
30ml/2 tbsp chopped fresh coriander
   (cilantro)
fresh coriander (cilantro) sprig,
   to garnish
pitta bread and Cucumber Raita, to serve

4 Stir-fry the vegetables for 5–7 minutes until the onions have browned.

5 Stir in the tuna, fresh chilli and grated ginger and cook for 5 minutes more.

6 Add the garam masala, lemon juice and fresh coriander and continue to cook for a further 3–4 minutes. Serve in warmed pitta bread with the Cucumber Raita, garnished with fresh coriander.

1 Thinly slice the onion and the red and green peppers. Set aside.

2 Heat the oil in a wok, karahi or large pan over a medium heat and fry the cumin seeds for 30–40 seconds until they begin to splutter.

3 Add the ground cumin and coriander, chilli powder and salt to the pan. Cook for 2 minutes. Add the garlic, onion and peppers and increase the heat a little.

COOK'S TIP
Place the pitta bread on a grill (broiler) rack and grill (broil) until it puffs up. It will then be easy to split with a sharp knife.

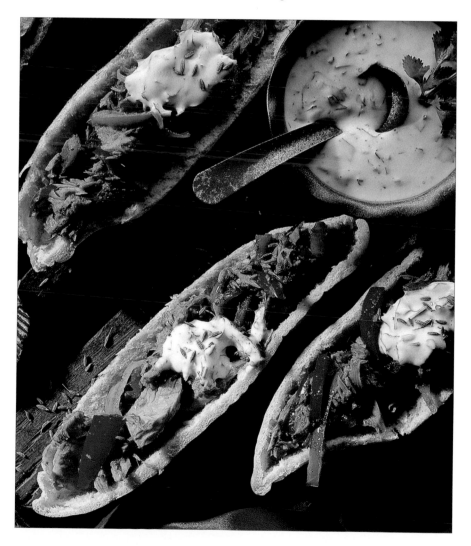

FISH STEW

Cooking fish with vegetables is very much a tradition in eastern regions. This hearty dish with potatoes, peppers and tomatoes is perfect served with breads such as chapatis or parathas. You can try other combinations, such as green beans and spinach, but you do need a starchy vegetable in order to thicken the sauce.

SERVES 4

30ml/2 tbsp vegetable oil
5ml/1 tsp cumin seeds
1 onion, chopped
1 red (bell) pepper, thinly sliced
1 garlic clove, crushed
2 fresh red chillies, finely chopped
2 bay leaves
2.5ml/½ tsp salt
5ml/1 tsp ground cumin
5ml/1 tsp ground coriander
5ml/1 tsp chilli powder
400g/14oz can chopped tomatoes
2 large potatoes, cut into 2.5cm/1in chunks
300ml/½ pint/1¼ cups fish stock
4 cod fillets
chapatis, to serve

1 Heat the oil in a wok, karahi or large pan over a medium heat and fry the cumin seeds for 30–40 seconds until they begin to splutter. Add the onion, red pepper, garlic, chillies and bay leaves and fry for 5–7 minutes more until the onions have browned.

2 Add the salt, ground cumin, ground coriander and chilli powder and cook for 1–2 minutes.

COOK'S TIP
Avoid reheating this dish. Serve it as soon as it is cooked because cod flesh flakes very easily. If preparing in advance, follow the recipe up to the end of step 3, then cover the sauce and store in the refrigerator. Cook step 4 before serving.

3 Stir in the tomatoes, potatoes and fish stock. Bring to the boil and simmer for a further 10 minutes, or until the potatoes are almost tender.

4 Add the fish fillets, then cover the pan and allow to simmer for 5–6 minutes until the fish is just cooked. Serve hot with chapatis, if you like.

FISH in a RICH TOMATO and ONION SAUCE

It is difficult to imagine the cuisine of eastern India without fish. Bengal is as well known for its fish and shellfish dishes as Goa on the west coast. In both regions, coconut is used extensively, and the difference in the taste, as always, lies in the spicing. This onion-rich dish is known as kalia *in Bengal, and a firm-fleshed fish is essential.*

SERVES 4

675g/1½lb steaks of firm-textured fish
   such as tuna or monkfish, skinned
30ml/2 tbsp lemon juice
5ml/1 tsp salt
5ml/1 tsp ground turmeric
vegetable oil, for shallow frying
40g/1½ oz/½ cup plain (all-purpose) flour
2.5ml/¼ tsp ground black pepper
60ml/4 tbsp vegetable oil
10ml/2 tsp granulated sugar
1 large onion, finely chopped
15ml/1 tbsp grated fresh root ginger
15ml/1 tbsp crushed garlic
5ml/1 tsp ground coriander
2.5–5ml/½–1 tsp hot chilli powder
175g/6 oz canned chopped tomatoes,
   including the juice
300ml/½ pint/1¼ cups warm water
30ml/2 tbsp chopped fresh coriander
   (cilantro) leaves, to garnish
plain boiled rice, to serve

1 Cut the fish into 7.5cm/3in pieces and put into a large bowl. Add the lemon juice and sprinkle with half the salt and half the turmeric. Mix gently with your fingertips and set aside for 15 minutes.

2 Pour enough oil into a 23cm/9in frying pan to cover the base to a depth of 1cm/½in and heat over a medium setting. Mix the flour and pepper and dust the fish in the seasoned flour. Add to the oil in a single layer and fry until browned on both sides and a light crust has formed. Drain on kitchen paper.

3 In a wok, karahi or large pan, heat 60ml/4 tbsp oil. When the oil is hot, but not smoking, add the sugar and let it caramelize. As soon as the sugar is brown, add the onion, ginger and garlic and fry for 7–8 minutes, until just beginning to colour. Stir regularly.

4 Add the ground coriander, chilli powder and the remaining turmeric. Stir-fry for about 30 seconds and add the tomatoes. Cook until the tomatoes are mushy and the oil separates from the spice paste, stirring regularly.

5 Pour the warm water and remaining salt into the pan, and bring to the boil. Carefully add the fried fish, reduce the heat to low and simmer, uncovered, for 5–6 minutes. Transfer to a serving dish and garnish with the coriander leaves. Serve with plain boiled rice.

COOK'S TIP
Like all ground spices, ground turmeric will lose its potency on keeping. Buy only small quantities, and store the powder in an airtight container, in a cupboard away from strong light.

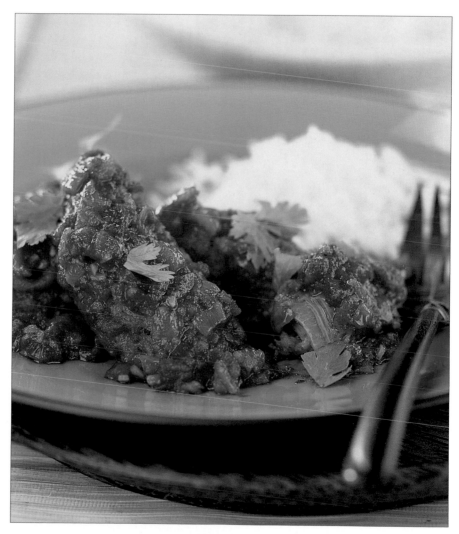

PRAWN CURRY

The Bay of Bengal provides Bengal and Orissa with enormous quantities of fish and shellfish. Eating plenty of fish, greens, lentils and peas is a way of life here. The food is generally cooked in mustard oil, which lends a distinctive, nutty flavour to the final dish.

SERVES 4

675g/1½lb raw tiger prawns (jumbo shrimp)
4 dried red chillies
50g/2oz/1 cup desiccated (dry, unsweetened, shredded) coconut
5ml/1 tsp black mustard seeds
1 large onion, chopped
45ml/3 tbsp vegetable oil
4 bay leaves
2.5cm/1in piece fresh root ginger, chopped
2 garlic cloves, crushed
15ml/1 tbsp ground coriander
5ml/1 tsp chilli powder
5ml/1 tsp salt
4 tomatoes, finely chopped
plain boiled rice, to serve

1 Peel the prawns. Run a sharp knife along the back of each prawn to make a shallow cut and carefully remove the thin black intestinal vein. You might like to leave a few of the prawns unpeeled, setting them aside to use as a garnish for the finished dish.

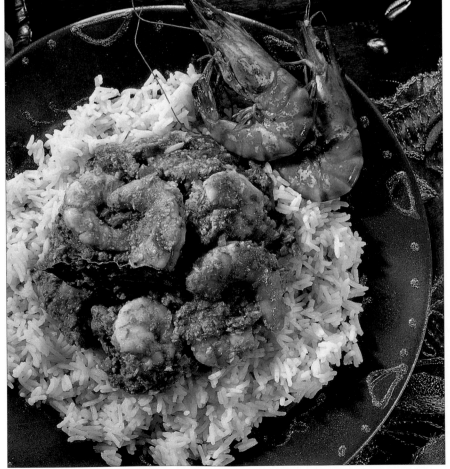

2 Put the dried red chillies, coconut, mustard seeds and onion in a wok, karahi or large pan and dry-fry over a medium heat for 5–6 minutes, or until the mixture begins to brown. Stir continuously to ensure even browning and to avoid burning the coconut. Put into a food processor or blender and process to a coarse paste.

3 Heat the vegetable oil in the pan and fry the bay leaves for 1 minute. Add the chopped ginger and the garlic, and fry for 2–3 minutes.

4 Add the ground coriander, chilli powder, salt and the paste and fry for about 5 minutes.

5 Stir in the tomatoes and about 175ml/6fl oz/¾ cup water and simmer for 5–6 minutes or until thickened.

6 Add the prawns and cook for about 4–5 minutes, or until they turn pink. Grill (broil) the reserved whole prawns, if using, until pink. Serve the curry on a ring of plain boiled rice and garnish with the whole prawns, if using.

KING PRAWN KORMA

Prawns are the most popular shellfish in Bengal. This dish is cooked in the style of malai chingri, *which means prawns cooked in dairy or coconut cream. Because of the richness of the ingredients, serve plain boiled rice with this korma.*

SERVES 4

10–12 peeled, cooked king prawns
   (jumbo shrimp), thawed if frozen
45ml/3 tbsp natural (plain) yogurt
5ml/1 tsp paprika
5ml/1 tsp garam masala
15ml/1 tbsp tomato purée (paste)
60ml/4 tbsp coconut milk
5ml/1 tsp chilli powder
150ml/¼ pint/⅔ cup water
15ml/1 tbsp vegetable oil
5ml/1 tsp crushed garlic
5ml/1 tsp grated fresh root ginger
2.5cm/1in piece cinnamon stick, halved
2 green cardamom pods
salt
15ml/1 tbsp chopped fresh coriander
   (cilantro), to garnish

1 If the prawns had been frozen, drain thoroughly in a sieve (strainer) over a bowl to ensure that all excess liquid is removed before cooking.

2 Place the yogurt, paprika, garam masala, tomato purée, coconut milk, chilli powder and water into a large glass bowl, and season to taste with salt.

3 Blend the ingredients together. Set aside.

4 Heat the oil in a wok, karahi or large pan, add the garlic, ginger, cinnamon, cardamoms and season to taste with salt. Fry over a low heat for 1–2 minutes.

5 Pour in the spice mixture and bring to the boil, stirring occasionally.

6 Add the prawns and cook, stirring constantly, until the sauce starts to thicken. Garnish and serve.

FRAGRANT LAMB CURRY

Essentially a Muslim dish known as rezala, *this delectable recipe comes from Bengal where there is a tradition of Muslim cooking. This is a legacy left by the Muslim rulers during the Mogul era.*

SERVES 4

1 large onion, roughly chopped
10ml/2 tsp grated fresh root ginger
10ml/2 tsp crushed garlic
4–5 cloves
2.5ml/½ tsp black peppercorns
6 green cardamom pods
5cm/2in piece cinnamon stick, halved
8 lamb rib chops
60ml/4 tbsp vegetable oil
1 large onion, finely sliced
175ml/6fl oz/¾ natural (plain) yogurt
50g/2oz/¼ cup butter
2.5ml/1 tsp salt
2.5ml/½ tsp ground cumin
2.5ml/½ tsp hot chilli powder
2.5ml/½ tsp freshly grated nutmeg
2.5ml/½ tsp granulated sugar
15ml/1 tbsp lime juice
pinch of saffron, steeped in 15ml/1 tbsp
    hot water for 10–15 minutes
15ml/1 tbsp rose water
rose petals, to garnish

1 Process the onion in a blender or food processor. Add a little water if necessary to form a purée.

2 Put the purée in a glass bowl and add the grated ginger, crushed garlic, cloves, peppercorns, cardamom pods, and cinnamon. Mix well.

3 Put the lamb chops in a large shallow glass dish and add the spice mixture. Mix thoroughly, cover the bowl and leave the lamb to marinate for 3–4 hours or overnight in the refrigerator. Bring back to room temperature before cooking.

4 In a wok, karahi or large pan, heat the oil over a medium-high heat and fry the sliced onion for 6–7 minutes, until golden brown. Remove the onion slices with a slotted spoon, squeezing out as much oil as possible on the side of the pan. Drain the onions on kitchen paper.

5 In the remaining oil, fry the marinated lamb chops for 4–5 minutes, stirring frequently. Reduce the heat to low, cover and cook for 5–7 minutes.

6 Meanwhile, mix the yogurt and butter together in a small pan and place over a low heat. Cook for 5–6 minutes, stirring constantly, then stir into the lamb chops along with the salt. Add the cumin and chilli powder and cover the pan. Cook for 45–50 minutes until the chops are tender.

7 Add the nutmeg and sugar, cook for 1–2 minutes and add the lime juice, saffron and rose water. Stir and mix well, simmer for 2–3 minutes and remove from the heat. Garnish with the fried onion and rose petals. Serve with naan bread or boiled basmati rice, if you like.

MASALA CHANNA

This is a typical Calcutta street food known as ghughni. Plates full of ghughni, with the wholesome taste of chickpeas laced with spices and tamarind juice, are enjoyed with flat breads such as chapatis and parathas.

SERVES 4

225g/8oz/1¼ cups dried chickpeas
50g/2oz tamarind pulp
120ml/4fl oz/½ cup boiling water
45ml/3 tbsp vegetable oil
2.5ml/½ tsp cumin seeds
1 onion, finely chopped
2 garlic cloves, crushed
2.5cm/1in piece fresh root ginger, grated
1 fresh green chilli, finely chopped
5ml/1 tsp ground cumin
5ml/1 tsp ground coriander
1.5ml/¼ tsp ground turmeric
2.5ml/½ tsp salt
225g/8oz tomatoes, skinned and
    finely chopped
2.5ml/½ tsp garam masala
chopped chillies and chopped onion,
    to garnish

1 Put the chickpeas in a large bowl and cover with plenty of cold water. Leave to soak overnight.

2 Drain the chickpeas and place in a large pan with double the volume of cold water. Bring to the boil and boil vigorously for 10 minutes. Skim off any scum, then cover and simmer for 1½–2 hours or until soft.

3 Meanwhile, break up the tamarind pulp and soak in the boiling water for about 15 minutes. Use the back of a spoon to rub the tamarind through a sieve (strainer) into a bowl, discarding any stones and fibre. (Leave out this step if you are using commercial tamarind paste in place of the fresh pulp.)

4 Heat the vegetable oil in a wok, karahi or large pan and fry the cumin seeds for 2 minutes until they begin to splutter. Add the chopped onion, garlic, ginger and chilli and fry for 5 minutes.

5 Add the cumin, coriander, turmeric and salt and fry for 3–4 minutes. Add the tomatoes and tamarind juice. Bring to the boil and simmer for 5 minutes.

6 Add the chickpeas and garam masala, cover and simmer for about 15 minutes. Garnish with the chillies and onion.

COOK'S TIP
Make double the quantity of tamarind juice and freeze in ice-cube trays. It will keep for up to 12 months. Alternatively, buy tamarind paste sold in Indian stores. It is ready to use and will keep for an indefinite period at room temperature.

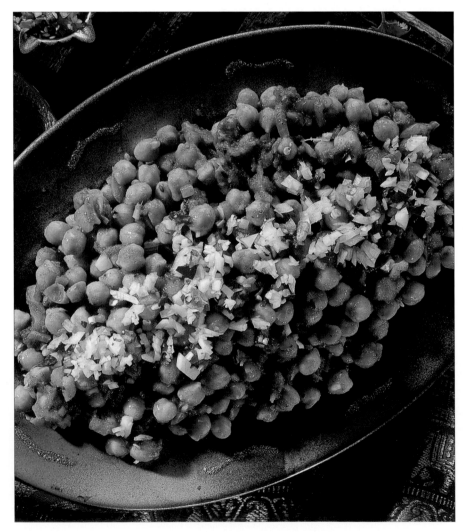

MIXED VEGETABLE CURRY

Curries based on a variety of vegetables are cooked throughout India, but they all differ from one another according to the spicing and the method of cooking. This particular version, made with onion seeds, is a typical example from the east and north-east of the country, where the dish is known as chorchori.

SERVES 4–6

350g/12oz mixed vegetables such as green
  beans, peas, potatoes, cauliflower,
  carrots, cabbage, mangetouts (snow
  peas) and button (white) mushrooms
30ml/2 tbsp vegetable oil
2.5ml/½ tsp mustard seeds
5ml/1 tsp cumin seeds, freshly roasted
2.5ml/½ tsp onion seeds
5ml/1 tsp ground turmeric
2 garlic cloves, crushed
6–8 curry leaves
1 dried red chilli
5ml/1 tsp granulated sugar
150ml/¼ pint/⅔ cup natural (plain) yogurt
  mixed with 5ml/1 tsp cornflour
  (cornstarch), well beaten
salt
fresh bay leaves, to garnish

1 Prepare all the vegetables you have chosen: string the beans; cube the potatoes; cut the cauliflower into florets; dice the carrots; shred the cabbage; trim the mangetouts; wash the mushrooms and leave them whole.

2 Heat a large, deep-sided pan with enough water to cook all the vegetables and bring to the boil. First add the potatoes and carrots and cook until nearly tender then add all the other vegetables and cook until nearly tender but still firm. All the vegetables should be only just tender except the potatoes, which should be tender. Drain well.

COOK'S TIP
If you have gram flour (besan), mix this with the yogurt instead of cornflour. It prevents the yogurt from curdling and lends a nutty taste.

3 Heat the oil in a large pan and add the mustard and cumin seeds. As they pop, add the remaining spices and fry gently until the garlic is golden and the chilli nearly burnt. Reduce the heat.

4 Fold in the drained vegetables, add the sugar and salt and gradually add the yogurt mixed with the cornflour. Heat through and serve immediately, garnished with fresh bay leaves.

CRISP FRIED AUBERGINE

The vegetarian community in Bengal would happily eat begun bhaja, *fried aubergine, and a lentil dish with rice for a main meal. Choose the large variety of aubergine with an unblemished, glossy skin. There is no need to soak the aubergine in salted water as today's aubergines generally have less bitterness in the skin than they used to.*

2 Halve the aubergine lengthwise and cut each half into 5mm/¼in thick slices. Rinse them and shake off the excess water, but do not pat dry. With some of the water still clinging to the slices, add them to the spiced gram flour mixture. Toss them around until they are evenly coated with the flour. Use a spoon if necessary to ensure that all the flour is incorporated.

3 Heat the oil in a deep-fat fryer or other suitable pan over a medium-high heat. If you have a thermometer, check that the oil has reached 190°C/375°F. Alternatively, drop a small piece of day-old bread into the oil. If it floats immediately, then the oil has reached the right temperature.

SERVES 4

50g/2oz/½ cup gram flour (besan)
15ml/1tbsp semolina or ground rice
2.5ml/½ tsp onion seeds
5ml/1 tsp cumin seeds
2.5ml/½ tsp fennel seeds or aniseeds
2.5–5ml/½–1 tsp hot chilli powder
2.5ml/½ tsp salt, or to taste
1 large aubergine (eggplant)
vegetable oil, for deep-frying

COOK'S TIP
Fennel and aniseeds aid digestion, and most deep-fried Indian recipes use them.

1 Sieve the gram flour into a large mixing bowl and add the remaining ingredients except the aubergine and the vegetable oil.

4 Fry the spice-coated aubergine slices in a single layer. Avoid overcrowding the pan as this will lower the oil temperature, resulting in a soggy texture. Fry until the aubergines are crisp and well browned. Drain on kitchen paper and serve with a chutney.

SWEET-and-SOUR PINEAPPLE

This may sound like a Chinese recipe, but it is a traditional Bengali dish known as tok.
The predominant flavour is ginger, and the pieces of golden pineapple, dotted with plump,
juicy raisins have plenty of visual appeal with a taste to match. It is equally delicious if
made with mangoes instead of the pineapple. Serve as a side dish or digestive.

SERVES 4

800g/1¾lb pineapple rings or chunks
  in natural juice
15ml/1 tbsp vegetable oil
2.5ml/½ tsp black mustard seeds
2.5ml/½ tsp cumin seeds
2.5ml/½ tsp onion seeds
10ml/2 tsp grated fresh root ginger
5ml/1 tsp crushed dried chillies
50g/2oz/⅓ cup seedless raisins
125g/4oz/⅔ cup granulated sugar
7.5ml/1½ tsp salt

3 Add the pineapple, raisins, sugar and salt. Add 300 ml/½ pint/1¼ cups of the juice (make up with cold water if necessary) and add to the pineapple.

VARIATION
Two or three mangoes can be used for this dish instead of the pineapple, if you prefer. Choose ripe fruits that will be full of flavour. To prepare, cut off both sides of the fruit, keeping close to the stone, then peel off the skin and chop the flesh into chunks. Canned mangoes in natural juice could also be used.

4 Bring the mixture to the boil, reduce the heat to medium and cook, uncovered, for 20–25 minutes.

1 Drain the pineapple in a sieve (strainer) and reserve the juice. Chop the pineapple rings or chunks finely (you should have approximately 500g/1¼lb).

2 Heat the vegetable oil in a wok, karahi or large pan over a medium heat and immediately add the mustard seeds. As soon as they pop, add the cumin seeds, then the onion seeds. Add the ginger and chillies and stir-fry the spices briskly for 30 seconds until they release their flavours.

POTATOES with ROASTED POPPY SEEDS

Poppy seeds are used in Indian cooking as thickening agents, and to lend a nutty taste to sauces. It is the creamy white variety of poppy seed that is used here, rather than the ones with a blue-grey hue that are used for baking.

SERVES 4

45ml/3 tbsp white poppy seeds
45–60ml/3–4 tbsp vegetable oil
675g/1½lb potatoes, peeled and cut into
   1cm/½in cubes
2.5ml/½ tsp black mustard seeds
2.5ml/½ tsp onion seeds
2.5ml/½ tsp cumin seeds
2.5ml/½ tsp fennel seeds
1–2 dried red chillies, chopped or broken
   into small pieces
2.5ml/½ tsp ground turmeric
2.5ml/½ tsp salt
150ml/¼ pint/⅔ cup warm water
fresh coriander (cilantro) sprigs, to garnish
pooris and natural (plain) yogurt, to serve

1 Preheat a wok, karahi or large pan over a medium setting. When the pan is hot, reduce the heat slightly and add the poppy seeds. Stir them around in the pan until they are just a shade darker. Remove from the pan and allow to cool.

2 In the pan, heat the vegetable oil over a medium heat and fry the cubes of potatoes until they are light brown. Remove them with a slotted spoon and drain on kitchen paper.

COOK'S TIP
Do not allow the dried chillies to burn or they will become bitter. Remove them from the pan when they have blackened.

3 To the same oil, add the mustard seeds. As soon as they begin to pop, add the onion, cumin and fennel seeds and the chillies. Let the chillies blacken.

4 Stir in the turmeric and follow quickly with the fried potatoes and salt. Stir well and add the warm water. Cover the pan with the lid and reduce the heat to low. Cook for 8–10 minutes, or until the potatoes are tender.

5 Grind the cooled poppy seeds in a pestle and mortar or coffee grinder. Stir the ground seeds into the potatoes. It should form a thick paste which should cling to the potatoes. If there is too much liquid, continue to stir over a medium heat until you have the right consistency. Transfer to a serving dish. Garnish with coriander and serve with pooris and natural yogurt.

COOK'S TIP
As they are ground, poppy seeds release a natural oil, which may prevent the blade of a spice mill or coffee grinder from moving. Scrape away anything that sticks to the blades and start again.

SPINACH with GOLDEN POTATOES

*The combination of spinach and potato is generally known as aloo saag or saag aloo.
As with most Indian dishes, there are different versions using the same or similar
ingredients. This recipe is from Bengal, where it is known as palong saaker ghonto.*

SERVES 4–6

450g/1lb spinach
30ml/2 tbsp vegetable oil
5ml/1 tsp black mustard seeds
1 onion, thinly sliced
2 garlic cloves, crushed
2.5cm/1in piece fresh root ginger,
    finely chopped
675g/1½lb firm potatoes, cut into
    2.5cm/1in chunks
5ml/1 tsp chilli powder
5ml/1 tsp salt
120ml/4fl oz/½ cup water

1 Blanch the spinach in boiling water
for 3–4 minutes, then drain in a sieve
(strainer) and leave to cool. When it is
cool enough to handle, squeeze out any
remaining liquid using the back of a
wooden spoon or with your hands.

2 Heat the oil in a large pan over a
medium heat and fry the mustard seeds
until they begin to splutter.

3 Add the sliced onion, crushed garlic
and chopped ginger and fry for about
5 minutes, stirring.

4 Stir in the potatoes, chilli powder,
salt and water and cook for 8 minutes,
stirring occasionally.

VARIATION
For an excellent alternative to spinach,
use 450g/1lb spring greens.

5 Add the spinach to the pan. Cover
and simmer for 10–15 minutes until the
potatoes are tender. Serve.

COOK'S TIP
Enhance the flavour by adding fresh red
chillies in step 3. Omit the chilli powder.

CHANA DHAL and BOTTLE GOURD CURRY

Chana dhal, also known as Bengal gram, is a very small type of chickpea grown in India. It has a nutty taste and gives fabulous earthy flavour to the food. Chana dhal is available from good Indian stores. Yellow split peas make a good substitute in terms of appearance and require the same cooking time, but the flavour is not quite the same.

SERVES 4–6

175g/6oz/⅔ cup chana dhal or yellow
   split peas, washed
450ml/¾ pint/scant 2 cups water
60ml/4 tbsp vegetable oil
2 fresh green chillies, chopped
1 onion, chopped
2 cloves garlic, crushed
5cm/2in piece fresh root ginger, grated
6–8 curry leaves
5ml/1 tsp chilli powder
5ml/1 tsp ground turmeric
450g/1lb bottle gourd or marrow (large
   zucchini), courgettes (zucchini), squash
   or pumpkin, peeled, pithed and sliced
60ml/4 tbsp tamarind juice
2 tomatoes, chopped
salt
a handful fresh coriander (cilantro) leaves,
   chopped

2 Heat the oil in a large pan and fry the chillies, onion, garlic, ginger, curry leaves, chilli powder and turmeric and salt until the onions have softened. Add the gourd (or other vegetable) pieces and mix.

3 Add the chana dhal and water and bring to the boil. Add the tamarind juice, tomatoes and coriander. Simmer until the gourd is cooked. Serve hot with a dry meat curry.

1 In a large pan, cook the chana dhal in the water, seasoned with salt, for about 30 minutes until the chana dhal grains are tender but not mushy. Put aside without draining away any excess water.

COOK'S TIP
If using courgettes (zucchini), add them along with the tamarind juice, tomatoes and coriander in step 3. Courgettes need much less cooking time than the other vegetables in the recipe.

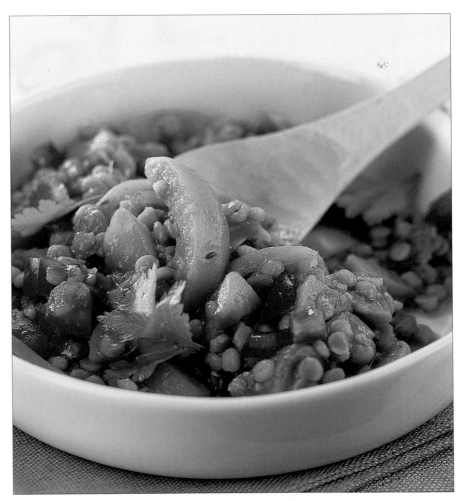

TARKA DHAL

Tarka, also spelt tadka, *is a hot oil seasoning that is folded into a dish before serving. In an Indian household, dhal is cooked every day and for most family meals a much simpler version is made.* Tarka dhal *is commonly found in Bengal, Assam and Bangladesh and it is the combination of spices that gives away its origin.*

SERVES 4–6

115g/4oz/½ cup red lentils, washed
50g/2oz/¼ cup chana dhal or
   yellow split peas, washed
600ml/1 pint/2½ cups water
5ml/1 tsp grated fresh root ginger
5ml/1 tsp crushed garlic
2.5ml/¼ tsp ground turmeric
2 fresh green chillies, chopped
7.5ml/1½ tsp salt

For the tarka
30ml/2 tbsp vegetable oil
1 onion, sliced
2.5ml/¼ tsp mixed mustard and onion
   seeds
4 dried red chillies
1 tomato, sliced

To garnish
15ml/1 tbsp chopped fresh coriander
   (cilantro), 1–2 fresh green chillies,
   seeded and sliced, 15ml/1 tbsp
   chopped mint

1 Pick over the washed chana dhal or lentils for any stones, then place in a large pan and boil in the water with the ginger, garlic, turmeric and chopped green chillies for 15–20 minutes or until the lentils are soft.

2 Mash the lentils with the back of a spoon until they are of the same consistency as chicken soup. If the mixture looks too dry, add a little more water.

3 To prepare the tarka, heat the oil in another pan and fry the onion with the mustard and onion seeds, dried red chillies and sliced tomato for 2 minutes.

4 Pour the tarka over the dhal in the frying pan and garnish with the chopped fresh coriander, fresh green chillies and chopped mint. Serve.

SOUTH INDIA

The food in the southern states is light and refreshing, with plenty of
fish and shellfish; it is also fiery, with much use being made of the
chillies that are grown throughout the region. In south India, coconut
milk is used to enrich sauces in place of the dairy cream and nuts
used in the north.

MUGHLAI-STYLE CHICKEN

The cuisine of Andhra Pradesh is renowned for its pungency because the hottest variety of chilli is grown there. In sharp contrast, however, the region is also home to the subtle flavours of a style of cooking known as nizami, *which has a distinct Mogul influence. This recipe, with the heady aroma of saffron and the captivating flavour of a silky almond and cream sauce, is a typical example.*

SERVES 4–6

4 chicken breast fillets, rubbed with
   a little garam masala
2 eggs, beaten with salt and pepper
90ml/6 tbsp ghee or vegetable oil
1 large onion, finely chopped
5cm/2in piece fresh root ginger,
   finely crushed
4 garlic cloves, finely crushed
4 cloves
4 green cardamom pods
5cm/2in piece cinnamon stick
2 bay leaves
15–20 saffron threads
150ml/¼ pint/⅔ cup natural (plain)
   yogurt, beaten with 5ml/1 tsp
   cornflour (cornstarch)
75ml/5 tbsp/⅓ cup double (heavy) cream
50g/2oz ground almonds
salt

3 Return the chicken to the pan, along with any juices, and gently cook until the chicken is tender. Adjust the seasoning if necessary.

4 Just before serving, fold in the double cream and ground almonds. Make sure the curry is piping hot before serving. Tricolour Pulao goes well with this dish.

1 Brush the chicken fillets with the beaten eggs. In a wok, karahi or large pan, heat the ghee or vegetable oil and fry the chicken until cooked through and browned on both sides. Remove the chicken from the pan and keep warm.

2 In the same pan, fry the chopped onion, ginger, garlic, cloves, cardamom pods, cinnamon and bay leaves. When the onion turns golden, remove the pan from the heat, allow the contents to cool a little and add the saffron and natural yogurt. Mix well to prevent the yogurt from curdling.

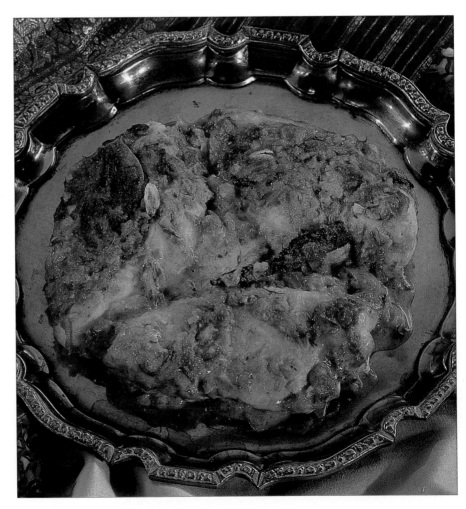

CHICKEN MADRAS

Madras, one of India's largest cities, is the capital of Tamil Nadu. The city is generally regarded as the heartland of southern Indian cuisine. It is surrounded by long stretches of beautiful beaches, shared between the Bay of Bengal to the east and the Indian Ocean to the south. The food is mainly vegetarian, but the small Muslim and Christian communities have a wonderful range of meat- and poultry-based dishes, such as this one.

SERVES 4

450g/1lb chicken breast fillets, skinned
45ml/3 tbsp tomato purée (paste)
large pinch ground fenugreek
1.5ml/¼ tsp ground fennel seeds
5ml/1 tsp grated fresh root ginger
7.5ml/1½ tsp ground coriander
5ml/1 tsp crushed garlic
5ml/1 tsp chilli powder
1.5ml/¼ tsp ground turmeric
30ml/2 tbsp lemon juice
5ml/1 tsp salt
300ml/½ pint/1¼ cups water
45ml/3 tbsp vegetable oil
2 onions, diced
2–4 curry leaves
2 fresh green chillies, seeded
    and chopped
15ml/1 tbsp chopped fresh coriander
    (cilantro), plus extra sprigs to garnish
naan bread, to serve

1 Cut the chicken breast fillets into cubes. Mix the tomato purée in a bowl with the fenugreek, fennel, ginger, ground coriander, garlic, chilli powder, turmeric, lemon juice, salt and water.

2 Heat the oil in a wok, karahi or large pan and fry the onions with the curry leaves until the onions are golden. Add the chicken and stir for 1 minute to seal.

COOK'S TIP
Take care not to use too much ground fenugreek, as it can be quite bitter.

3 Pour the tomato sauce and spice mixture into the pan. Stir for 2 minutes to ensure the ingredients are well mixed.

4 Lower the heat and cook for 8–10 minutes, then add the chillies and fresh coriander. Garnish and serve.

MADRAS BEEF CURRY

Although Madras is renowned for the best vegetarian food in the country, meat-based recipes such as this one are also extremely popular. This particular recipe is a contribution by the area's small Muslim community.

SERVES 4–6

60ml/4 tbsp vegetable oil
1 large onion, finely sliced
3–4 cloves
4 green cardamoms
2 whole star anise
4 fresh green chillies, chopped
2 fresh or dried red chillies, chopped
45ml/3 tbsp Madras masala paste
5ml/1 tsp ground turmeric
450g/1lb lean beef, cubed
60ml/4 tbsp tamarind juice
granulated sugar, to taste
salt
a few fresh coriander (cilantro) leaves, chopped, to garnish

1 Heat the vegetable oil in a wok, karahi or large pan over a medium heat and fry the onion slices for 8–9 minutes until they turn golden brown. Lower the heat, add all the spice ingredients, and fry for a further 2–3 minutes.

2 Add the beef and mix well. Cover and cook on low heat until the beef is tender. Cook uncovered on a higher heat for the last few minutes to reduce any excess liquid.

COOK'S TIP
To tenderize the meat, add 60ml/4 tbsp white wine vinegar in step 2, along with the meat, and omit the tamarind juice.

3 Fold in the tamarind juice, sugar and salt. Reheat the dish and garnish with the chopped coriander leaves. Tricolour Pulao and Tomato and Onion Salad would both make excellent accompaniments to this dish.

CHILLI MEAT with CURRY LEAVES

Curry leaves and chillies are two of the hallmark ingredients used in the southern states of India. This recipe is from the state of Andhra Pradesh, where the hottest chillies, known as Guntur after the region where they are produced, are grown in abundance.

SERVES 4–6

30ml/2 tbsp vegetable oil
1 large onion, finely sliced
5cm/2in piece fresh root ginger, grated
4 garlic cloves, crushed
12 curry leaves
45ml/3 tbsp extra hot curry paste, or
   60ml/4 tbsp hot curry powder
15ml/1 tbsp chilli powder
5ml/1 tsp five-spice powder
5ml/1 tsp ground turmeric
900g/2lb lean lamb, beef or pork, cubed
175ml/6fl oz/¾ cup thick coconut milk
salt
red onion, finely sliced, to garnish
Indian bread and Fruit Raita, to serve

1 Heat the oil in a wok, karahi or large, pan, and fry the onion, ginger, garlic and curry leaves until the onion is soft. Add the curry paste or powder, chilli and five-spice powder, turmeric and salt.

2 Add the meat and stir well over a medium heat to seal and evenly brown the meat pieces. Keep stirring until the oil separates. Cover the pan and cook for about 20 minutes.

COOK'S TIP
For extra flavour, reserve half the curry leaves and add in step 3, along with the coconut milk.

3 Stir in the coconut milk and simmer, covered, until the meat is cooked. Towards the end of cooking, uncover the pan to reduce the excess liquid. Garnish and serve with any Indian bread, and with Fruit Raita, for a cooling effect.

LAMB KORMA

*Although south Indian food is generally free of foreign influences, the city of Hyderabad
in Andhra Pradesh has a rich heritage of Mogul cuisine. It was here that the last of the
Mogul emperors retired before finally handing over power to the Nizam dynasty.*

SERVES 4–6

15ml/1 tbsp white sesame seeds
15ml/1 tbsp white poppy seeds
50g/2oz/½ cup blanched almonds
2 fresh green chillies, seeded
6 garlic cloves, sliced
5cm/2in piece fresh root ginger, sliced
1 onion, finely chopped
45ml/3 tbsp ghee or vegetable oil
6 green cardamom pods
5cm/2in piece cinnamon stick
4 cloves
900g/2lb lean lamb, boned and cubed
5ml/1 tsp ground cumin
5ml/1 tsp ground coriander
300ml/½ pint/1¼ cups double (heavy)
    cream mixed with 2.5ml/½ tsp
    cornflour (cornstarch)
salt
roasted sesame seeds, to garnish

1 Preheat a wok, karahi or large pan
over a medium heat without any fat, and
add the first seven ingredients. Stir until
they begin to change colour. They should
go just a shade darker.

2 Allow the mixture to cool, then grind
to a fine paste using a pestle and mortar
or in a food processor. Heat the ghee or
oil in the pan over a low heat.

3 Fry the cardamoms, cinnamon and
cloves until the cloves swell. Add the
lamb, ground cumin and coriander and
the prepared paste, and season with salt,
to taste. Increase the heat to medium
and stir well. Reduce the heat to low,
then cover the pan and cook until the
lamb is almost done.

4 Remove from the heat, allow to cool
a little and gradually fold in the cream,
reserving 5ml/1 tsp to garnish. To serve,
gently reheat the lamb, uncovered.
Garnish with the sesame seeds and the
reserved cream. This korma is very good
served with Classic Pulao.

COOK'S TIP
If white poppy seeds are not available, use
sunflower seeds instead.

CAULIFLOWER in COCONUT SAUCE

Coconut is used for both sweet and savoury dishes in south Indian cooking. This versatile fruit with its many by-products, including coconut oil, which is widely used as a cooking medium, provides the basis for a huge manufacturing industry all over the southern states.

SERVES 4–6

15ml/1 tbsp gram flour (besan)
120ml/4fl oz/½ cup water
5ml/1 tsp chilli powder
15ml/1 tbsp ground coriander
5ml/1 tsp ground cumin
5ml/1 tsp mustard powder
5ml/1 tsp ground turmeric
60ml/4 tbsp vegetable oil
6–8 curry leaves
5ml/1 tsp cumin seeds
1 cauliflower, broken into florets
175ml/6fl oz/¾ cup thick coconut milk
juice of 2 lemons
salt
lime slices, to garnish

1 Mix the gram flour with a little water to make a smooth paste. Add the chilli, coriander, cumin, mustard, turmeric and salt. Add the remaining water and mix to blend the ingredients.

2 Heat the oil in a wok, karahi or large pan, and fry the curry leaves and the cumin seeds. Add the spice paste and simmer for about 5 minutes. If the sauce is too thick, add a little hot water.

COOK'S TIP

Serve this dish southern-style, with plain rice and Spiced Lentils with Spinach. If you prefer, serve a northern-style meal with parathas and Kashmiri Chicken Curry.

3 Add the cauliflower and coconut milk. Bring to the boil, reduce the heat, cover and cook until the cauliflower is tender but crunchy. Cook longer if you prefer. Add the lemon juice, mix throughly and serve hot, garnished with lime slices.

MARINATED FRIED FISH

Fish and shellfish are a strong feature of the cuisine in the coastal region of southern India. Kerala, in the southernmost tip of the country, produces some of the finest fish and shellfish dishes. These are flavoured with local spices, grown in the fabulous spice plantation that is the pride and joy of the state.

SERVES 4–6

1 small onion, coarsely chopped
4 garlic cloves, crushed
5cm/2in piece fresh root ginger, chopped
5ml/1 tsp ground turmeric
10ml/2 tsp chilli powder
4 red mullets or snappers
vegetable oil, for shallow frying
5ml/1 tsp cumin seeds
3 fresh green chillies, finely sliced
salt
lemon or lime wedges, to serve

COOK'S TIP
To enhance the flavour, add 15ml/1 tbsp chopped fresh coriander (cilantro) leaves to the spice paste in step 1.

1 In a food processor, grind the first five ingredients with salt to a smooth paste. Make several slashes on both sides of the fish and rub them with the paste. Leave to rest for 1 hour. Excess fluid will be released as the salt dissolves, so lightly pat the fish dry with kitchen paper without removing the paste.

2 Heat the oil and fry the cumin seeds and sliced chillies for 1 minute. Add the fish, in batches if necessary, and fry on one side. When the first side is sealed, turn them over very gently to ensure they do not break. Fry until golden brown on both sides, drain and serve hot, with lemon or lime wedges.

MIXED VEGETABLES IN COCONUT SAUCE

A vegetable dish is an essential part of an Indian meal, even for a simple occasion, where one or two vegetable dishes may be served with a lentil dhal, *a raita, and bread or boiled rice. There are many ways to make a vegetable curry, but this recipe, in which the vegetables are simmered in coconut milk, is typical of South India.*

SERVES 4

225g/8oz potatoes, cut into 5cm/2in cubes
125g/4oz/¾ cup French (green) beans
150g/5oz carrots, scraped and cut into
    5cm/2in cubes
500ml/17fl oz/2¼ cups hot water
1 small aubergine (eggplant), about
    225g/8oz, quartered lengthwise
75g/3oz coconut milk powder
5ml/1 tsp salt
30ml/2 tbsp vegetable oil
6–8 fresh or 8–10 dried curry leaves
1–2 dried red chillies, chopped into
    small pieces
5ml/1 tsp ground cumin
5ml/1 tsp ground coriander
2.5ml/½ tsp ground turmeric

1 Put the potatoes, beans and carrots in a large pan and add 300ml/½ pint/ 1¼ cups of the hot water and bring to the boil. Reduce the heat a little, cover the pan and cook for 5 minutes.

2 Cut the aubergine quarters into 5cm/2in pieces. Rinse. Add to the pan.

3 Blend the coconut milk powder with the remaining hot water and add to the vegetables, with the salt. Bring to a slow simmer, cover and cook for 6–7 minutes.

4 In a small pan heat the oil over a medium heat and add the curry leaves and the chillies. Immediately follow with the cumin, coriander and turmeric. Stir-fry the spices for 15–20 seconds and pour the entire contents of the pan over the vegetables. Stir to distribute the spices evenly and remove from the heat. Serve with any Indian bread.

STUFFED AUBERGINES in SEASONED TAMARIND JUICE

The traditional way of cooking with tamarind is in a terracotta dish, which brings out the full fruity tartness of the tamarind. This spicy aubergine dish will add a refreshing tang to any meal.

SERVES 4

12 baby aubergines (eggplant)
30ml/2 tbsp vegetable oil
1 small onion, chopped
10ml/2 tsp grated fresh root ginger
10ml/2 tsp crushed garlic
5ml/1 tsp coriander seeds
5ml/1 tsp cumin seeds
10ml/2 tsp white poppy seeds
10ml/2 tsp sesame seeds
10ml/2 tsp desiccated (dry, unsweetened, shredded) coconut
15ml/1 tbsp dry-roasted skinned peanuts
2.5–5ml/½–1 tsp chilli powder
5ml/1 tsp salt
6–8 curry leaves
1–2 dried red chillies, chopped
2.5ml/½ tsp concentrated tamarind paste

1 Make three deep slits lengthwise on each aubergine, without cutting through, then soak in salted water for 20 minutes.

2 Heat half the oil in a pan and sautée the onion for 3–4 minutes. Add the ginger and garlic and cook for 30 seconds.

3 Add the coriander and cumin seeds and sautée for 30 seconds, then add the poppy seeds, sesame seeds and coconut. Sautée for 1 minute, stirring constantly. Allow to cool slightly, then grind the spices in a food processor, adding 105ml/ 7 tbsp warm water. The mixture should resemble a thick, slightly coarse paste.

4 Mix the peanuts, chilli powder and salt into the spice paste. Drain the aubergines and dry on kitchen paper. Stuff each of the slits with the spice paste and reserve any remaining paste.

5 Heat the remaining oil in a wok, karahi or large pan over a medium heat and add the curry leaves and chillies. Let the chillies blacken, then add the aubergines and the tamarind blended with 105ml/ 7 tbsp hot water. Add any remaining spice paste and stir to mix.

6 Cover the pan and simmer gently for 15–20 minutes or until the aubergines are tender. Serve with chapatis and a meat or poultry dish, if you like.

POTATOES in CHILLI TAMARIND SAUCE

In this favourite potato dish from the state of Karnataka, the combination of chilli and tamarind awakens the taste buds immediately. This version adapts the traditional recipe slightly, to reduce the pungency and enhance the dish's fiery appearance.

SERVES 4–6

450g/1lb small new potatoes, washed
    and dried
25g/1oz whole dried red chillies,
    preferably Kashmiri
7.5ml/1½ tsp cumin seeds
4 garlic cloves
90ml/6 tbsp vegetable oil
60ml/4 tbsp thick tamarind juice
30ml/2 tbsp tomato purée (paste)
4 curry leaves
5ml/1 tsp granulated sugar
1.5ml/¼ tsp asafoetida
salt
coriander (cilantro) sprigs and lemon
    wedges, to garnish

1 Boil the potatoes until they are fully cooked, ensuring they do not break. To test, insert a thin sharp knife into the potatoes. It should come out clean when the potatoes are fully cooked. Drain and cool the potatoes in iced water to prevent further cooking.

2 Soak the chillies for 5 minutes in warm water. Drain and grind with the cumin seeds and garlic to a coarse paste either using a pestle and mortar or in a food processor.

COOK'S TIP
Chunks of sweet potatoes can be used as an alternative to new potatoes.

3 Heat the oil and fry the paste, tamarind juice, tomato purée, curry leaves, salt, sugar and asafoetida until the oil separates from the spice paste. Add the potatoes. Reduce the heat, cover and simmer for 5 minutes. Garnish and serve.

MASALA BEANS with FENUGREEK

The term masala *refers to the blending of several spices to achieve a distinctive taste, with different spice-combinations being used to complement specific ingredients. Households will traditionally create their own blends, and many are quite unique.*

SERVES 4

1 onion
5ml/1 tsp ground cumin
5ml/1 tsp ground coriander
5ml/1 tsp sesame seeds
5ml/1 tsp chilli powder
2.5ml/½ tsp crushed garlic
1.5ml/¼ tsp ground turmeric
5ml/1 tsp salt
30ml/2 tbsp vegetable oil
1 tomato, quartered
225g/8oz/1½ cups French (green) beans, blanched
1 bunch fresh fenugreek leaves, stems discarded
60ml/4 tbsp chopped fresh coriander (cilantro)
15ml/1 tbsp lemon juice

1 Roughly chop the onion. Mix together the cumin and coriander, sesame seeds, chilli powder, garlic, turmeric and salt.

2 Put the chopped onion and spice mixture into a food processor or blender, and process for 30–45 seconds until you have a rough paste.

3 In a wok, karahi or large pan, heat the oil over a medium heat and fry the spice paste for about 5 minutes, stirring the mixture occasionally.

VARIATION
Instead of fresh fenugreek, you can also use 15ml/1 tbsp dried fenugreek for this recipe. Dried fenugreek is readily available from Indian stores and markets. It may be sold by its Indian name, *kasuri methi*.

4 Add the tomato quarters, blanched French beans, fresh fenugreek and chopped coriander.

5 Stir-fry the contents of the pan for about 5 minutes, then sprinkle in the lemon juice and serve.

CHILLI and MUSTARD FLAVOURED PINEAPPLE

Pineapple is cooked with coconut milk and a blend of spices in this South Indian dish, which could be served with any meat, fish or vegetable curry. The chilli adds heat, and the mustard seeds lend a rich, nutty flavour that complements the sharpness of the pineapple, while the coconut milk provides a delectable creamy sweetness.

2 Put the pineapple in a wok, karahi or large pan and add the measured water, with the coconut milk, turmeric and crushed chillies. Bring to a slow simmer over a low heat, and cook, covered, for 10–12 minutes, or until the pineapple is soft, but not mushy.

3 Add the salt and sugar, and cook, uncovered, until the sauce thickens.

4 Heat the oil in a second pan, and add the mustard seeds. As soon as they begin to pop, add the cumin seeds and the onion. Fry for 6–7 minutes, stirring regularly, until the onion is soft.

5 Add the chillies and curry leaves. Fry for a further 1–2 minutes and pour the entire contents over the pineapple. Stir well, then remove from the heat. Serve hot or cold, but not chilled.

SERVES 4

1 pineapple
50ml/2fl oz/¼ cup water
150ml/¼ pint/⅔ cup can coconut milk
2.5ml/½ tsp ground turmeric
2.5ml/½ tsp crushed dried chillies
5ml/1 tsp salt
10ml/2 tsp granulated sugar
15ml/1 tbsp groundnut (peanut) oil
2.5ml/½ tsp mustard seeds
2.5ml/½ tsp cumin seeds
1 small onion, finely chopped
1–2 dried red chillies, broken
6–8 curry leaves

1 Halve the pineapple lengthwise and cut each half into two, so that you end up with four boat-shaped pieces. Peel them and remove the eyes and the central core. Cut into bitesize pieces.

COOK'S TIP

Use canned pineapple in natural juice to save time. You will need approximately 500g/1¼lb drained pineapple.

LENTILS SEASONED with GARLIC-INFUSED OIL

This recipe, known as sambhar, *varies considerably within the southern states. Vegetables are added to the lentils, and this can be a single vegetable or a combination of two or more. It is traditionally served with steamed rice dumplings (idlis) or stuffed rice pancakes (dosai). It is also extremely satisfying with plain boiled rice.*

SERVES 4–6

120ml/8 tbsp vegetable oil
2.5ml/½ tsp mustard seeds
2.5ml/½ tsp cumin seeds
2 dried red chillies
1.5ml/¼ tsp asafoetida
6–8 curry leaves
2 garlic cloves, crushed, plus 2 garlic
   cloves, sliced
30ml/2 tbsp desiccated (dry, unsweetened,
   shredded) coconut
225g/8oz/1 cup red lentils, picked over,
   washed and drained
10ml/2 tsp sambhar masala
2.5ml/½ tsp ground turmeric
450ml/¾ pint/scant 2 cups water
450g/1lb mixed vegetables, such as okra,
   courgettes (zucchini), aubergine
   (eggplant) cauliflower, shallots and
   (bell) peppers
60ml/4 tbsp tamarind juice
4 firm tomatoes, quartered
a few coriander (cilantro) leaves, chopped

1 Heat half the oil in a wok, karahi or large pan, and stir-fry the next seven ingredients until the coconut begins to brown. Stir in the prepared red lentils, sambhar masala and turmeric. Stir-fry for 2–3 minutes and add the water. Bring it to the boil and reduce the heat to low.

COOK'S TIP
Red lentils are used in this recipe, but the traditional choice would be yellow split lentils, known as toor dhal or tuvar dhal, which are available from Indian stores.

2 Cover the pan and leave to simmer for 25–30 minutes, until the lentils are mushy. Add the mixed vegetables, tamarind juice and tomato quarters. Cook until the vegetables are just tender.

3 Heat the remaining oil in a small pan over a low heat, and fry the garlic slices until golden. Stir in the coriander leaves, then pour over the lentils and vegetables. Mix at the table before serving.

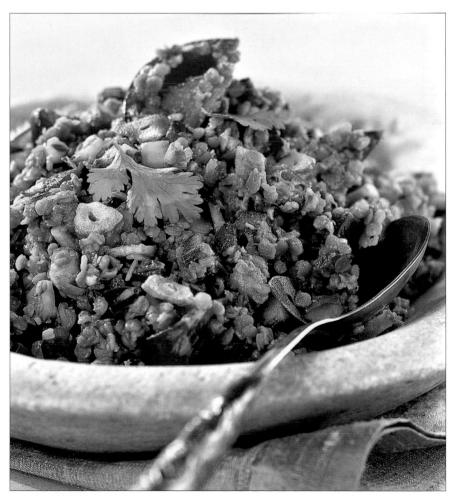

STUFFED BANANAS

Bananas are cooked with spices in many different ways in southern India. Some recipes contain large quantities of chillies, but the taste is skilfully mellowed by adding coconut milk and tamarind juice. Green bananas are available from Indian stores, or you can use plantains or unripe eating bananas that are firm to the touch.

SERVES 4

4 green bananas or plantains
30ml/2 tbsp ground coriander
15ml/1 tbsp ground cumin
5ml/1 tsp chilli powder
2.5ml/½ tsp salt
1.5ml/¼ tsp ground turmeric
5ml/1 tsp granulated sugar
15ml/1 tbsp gram flour (besan)
45ml/3 tbsp chopped fresh coriander
   (cilantro), plus extra sprigs
   to garnish
90ml/6 tbsp vegetable oil
1.5ml/¼ tsp cumin seeds
1.5ml/¼ tsp black mustard seeds

1 Trim the bananas or plantains and cut each crossways into three equal pieces, leaving the skin on. Make a lengthwise slit along each piece of banana, without cutting all the way through the flesh.

2 On a plate mix together the ground coriander, cumin, chilli powder, salt, turmeric, sugar, gram flour, chopped fresh coriander and 15ml/1 tbsp of the oil. Use your fingers to combine well.

3 Carefully stuff each piece of banana with the spice mixture, taking care not to break the bananas in half.

4 Heat the remaining oil in a wok, karahi or large pan, and fry the cumin and mustard seeds for 2 minutes or until they begin to splutter. Add the bananas and toss gently in the oil. Cover and simmer over a low heat for 15 minutes, stirring from time to time, until the bananas are soft but not mushy.

5 Garnish with the fresh coriander sprigs, and serve with warm chapatis, if you like. Other good accompaniments include Prawn Biryani and Spiced Yogurt.

COOK'S TIP
Baby courgettes (zucchini) would make a delicious alternative to bananas.

SPICED LENTILS with SPINACH

Spinach cooked with chana dhal *lentils makes a wholesome, healthy dish. It is perfect for a vegetarian diet, as it provides protein, vitamins and minerals in one dish. Serve it with naan bread, chapatis or plain boiled rice to make a satisfying main course. A salad or a chutney will add an extra special zest to the meal.*

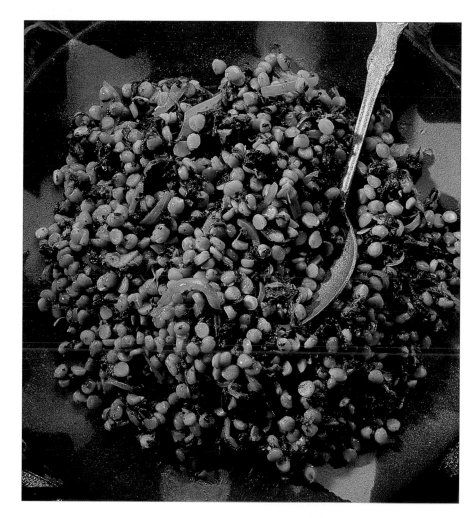

2 Drain the chana dhal or split peas and put in a large pan with the water. Bring to the boil, cover, and simmer for about 20–25 minutes until the dhal are soft. Cook, uncovered, until the cooking liquid has evaporated completely.

3 Heat the oil in a wok, karahi or large pan and fry the mustard seeds for about 2 minutes until they begin to splutter. Add the onion, garlic, ginger and chilli and fry for 5–6 minutes, then add the spinach and cook for 10 minutes or until the spinach is dry and the liquid is absorbed. Stir in the remaining spices and salt and cook for 2–3 minutes.

4 Add the chana dhal or split peas to the spinach in the pan and cook, stirring, for about 5 minutes. Serve hot with warm naan bread, or with plain boiled rice, if you like.

COOK'S TIP

Use canned chickpeas in place of chana dhal for a quick alternative. Drain, rinse in water, drain again, and add in step 4.

SERVES 4

175g/6oz/¾ cup chana dhal or yellow
   split peas
175ml/6fl oz/¾ cup water
30ml/2 tbsp vegetable oil
1.5ml/¼ tsp black mustard seeds
1 onion, thinly sliced
2 garlic cloves, crushed
2.5cm/1in piece fresh root ginger, grated
1 red chilli, finely chopped
275g/10oz frozen spinach, thawed
1.5ml/¼ tsp chilli powder
2.5ml/½ tsp ground coriander
2.5ml/½ tsp garam masala
2.5ml/½ tsp salt

1 Wash the chana dhal or split peas in several changes of cold water. Put the dhal or peas into a large bowl and cover with plenty of cold water. Leave to soak for about 30 minutes.

WEST INDIA

The western states of Gujarat and Maharashtra have developed

an excellent repertoire of vegetarian dishes, using fresh vegetables,

dairy products and lentils and peas. Goa, to the south of Mumbai,

formerly Bombay, shows Portuguese influences; its most famous

culinary export is vindaloo.

GOAN CHICKEN CURRY

Lines of swaying palm trees and the raised borders of a vast patchwork of paddy fields are just two of the features that constitute the superb landscape of Goa. Not surprisingly, coconut, in all of its forms, is widely used to enrich Goan cuisine.

SERVES 4

75g/3oz/1½ cups desiccated (dry, unsweetened, shredded) coconut
30ml/2 tbsp vegetable oil
2.5ml/½ tsp cumin seeds
4 black peppercorns
15ml/1 tbsp fennel seeds
15ml/1 tbsp coriander seeds
2 onions, finely chopped
2.5ml/½ tsp salt
8 small chicken pieces, such as thighs and drumsticks, skinned
fresh coriander (cilantro) sprigs and lemon wedges, to garnish

1 Put the desiccated coconut in a bowl with 45ml/3 tbsp water. Leave to soak for 15 minutes.

2 Heat 15ml/1 tbsp of the oil in a wok, karahi or large pan and fry the cumin seeds, peppercorns, fennel and coriander seeds over a low heat for 3–4 minutes until they begin to splutter.

COOK'S TIP
If you prefer, make the spiced coconut mixture the day before and chill it in the refrigerator, then continue from step 6 when required.

3 Add the finely chopped onions and fry for about 5 minutes, stirring occasionally, until the onion has softened and turned opaque.

4 Stir in the coconut, along with the soaking water and salt, and continue to fry for a further 5 minutes, stirring occasionally to prevent the mixture from sticking to the pan.

5 Put the coconut mixture into a food processor or blender and process to form a coarse paste. Spoon into a bowl and set aside until required.

6 Heat the remaining oil and fry the chicken for 10 minutes. Add the coconut paste and cook over a low heat for 15–20 minutes, or until the coconut mixture is golden brown and the chicken is tender.

7 Transfer the curry to a warmed serving plate, and garnish with sprigs of fresh coriander and lemon wedges. Mint and Coconut Chutney, plain boiled rice or a lentil dish would all make good accompaniments to this recipe.

CHICKEN with GREEN MANGO

Green or unripe mango is meant only for cooking purposes. These fruits are smaller than eating mangoes, and they have a sharper taste. They can be bought from Indian stores and markets, but if not available, cooking apples make an easy alternative.

SERVES 4

1 green (unripe) mango or cooking apple
450g/1lb chicken breast fillets, skinned
    and cubed
1.5ml/¼ tsp onion seeds
5ml/1 tsp grated fresh root ginger
2.5ml/½ tsp crushed garlic
5ml/1 tsp chilli powder
1.5ml/¼ tsp ground turmeric
5ml/1 tsp salt
5ml/1 tsp ground coriander
30ml/2 tbsp vegetable oil
2 onions, sliced
4 curry leaves
300ml/½ pint/1¼ cups water
2 tomatoes, quartered
2 fresh green chillies, chopped
30ml/2 tbsp chopped fresh
    coriander (cilantro)

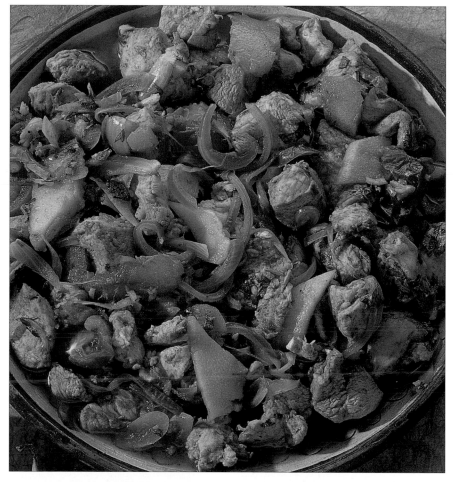

1 To prepare the mango, peel the skin and slice the flesh thickly. Discard the stone (pit) from the middle. Place the mango slices in a bowl, cover and set aside. If using apple, coat the slices with lemon juice to prevent discoloration.

2 Put the cubed chicken into a large mixing bowl and add the onion seeds, ginger, garlic, chilli powder, turmeric, salt and ground coriander. Mix the spices with the chicken, then stir in half the mango or apple slices.

3 Heat the oil in a wok, karahi or large pan over a medium heat, and fry the sliced onions until golden brown. Add the curry leaves to the pan, and stir very gently to release their flavour.

4 Gradually add the chicken to the pan, stirring all the time. Stir-fry briskly over a medium heat until the chicken is opaque.

5 Pour in the water, lower the heat and cook for 12–15 minutes, stirring, until the chicken is cooked through and the water has been completely absorbed.

6 Add the remaining mango or apple slices, the tomatoes, green chillies and fresh coriander. Plain boiled rice and Stuffed Okra are good accompaniments to serve with this dish.

VARIATION
Try fillets of rabbit for an unusual treat.

SAMOSAS

The origin of samosas can be attributed to the western states of Maharashtra and Gujarat, which are famous for these fabulous crispy pastries with spiced vegetable fillings. The original samosa is vegetarian, but meat fillings are also used, especially in northern India. In this recipe, ready-made spring roll pastry is used as a quick alternative.

MAKES 30

1 packet spring roll pastry, thawed and
    wrapped in a damp towel
vegetable oil, for deep-frying
Fresh Coriander Chutney, to serve

For the filling
3 large potatoes, boiled and mashed
75g/3oz/¾ cup frozen peas, thawed and
    cooked
50g/2oz/⅓ cup canned sweetcorn, drained
5ml/1 tsp ground coriander
5ml/1 tsp ground cumin
5ml/1 tsp amchur (dry mango powder)
1 small red onion, finely chopped
2 fresh green chillies, finely chopped
30ml/2 tbsp each fresh coriander (cilantro)
    and mint leaves, chopped
juice of 1 lemon
salt

1 Toss all the filling ingredients together in a large mixing bowl until well blended. Adjust the seasoning with salt and lemon juice, if necessary.

2 Working with one strip of pastry at a time, place 15ml/1 tbsp of the filling mixture at one end of the strip and diagonally fold the pastry to form a triangle. Repeat with the other strips.

3 Heat enough oil for deep-frying and fry the samosas in small batches until they are golden brown. Serve hot. Fresh Coriander Chutney or a chilli sauce are ideal for dipping.

COOK'S TIP
Filo pastry is an excellent alternative. Brush the filo samosas with oil and bake in a preheated hot oven for 25 minutes.

BEEF VINDALOO

Vindaloo is Goa's most famous export, but its origins are in fact Portuguese. In the 16th century, when Portuguese traders embarked on their long voyage to India, they carried pork, preserved in vinegar, garlic and black pepper. The word vin *comes from* vinegar *and* aloo *is derived from* alho, *the Portuguese word for garlic.*

SERVES 4

15ml/1 tbsp cumin seeds
4 dried red chillies
5ml/1 tsp black peppercorns
5 green cardamom pods, seeds only
5ml/1 tsp fenugreek seeds
5ml/1 tsp black mustard seeds
2.5ml/½ tsp salt
2.5ml/½ tsp demerara (raw) sugar
60ml/4 tbsp white wine vinegar
60ml/4 tbsp vegetable oil
1 large onion, finely chopped
900g/2lb stewing beef, cut into
   2.5cm/1in cubes
2.5cm/1in piece fresh root ginger, shredded
1 garlic clove, crushed
10ml/2 tsp ground coriander
2.5ml/½ tsp ground turmeric
plain and yellow rice, to serve

1 Use a pestle and mortar to grind the cumin seeds, chillies, peppercorns, cardamom seeds, fenugreek seeds and mustard seeds to a fine powder. Add the salt, sugar and white wine vinegar and mix to a thin paste.

2 Heat 30ml/2 tbsp of the oil and fry the onion over a medium heat for 8–10 minutes. Put the onion and the spice mixture into a food processor or blender and process to a coarse paste.

VARIATION
Pork tenderloin or leg is the traditional meat for vindaloo. If using leg, remove the crackling and trim off all visible fat.

3 Heat the remaining oil in the pan and fry the meat cubes over a medium heat for 10 minutes or until lightly browned. Remove the beef cubes with a slotted spoon and set aside.

4 Add the shredded ginger and crushed garlic to the pan and fry for 2 minutes. Stir in the coriander and turmeric and fry for 2 minutes more.

COOK'S TIP
To make plain and yellow rice, infuse (steep) a pinch of saffron threads or dissolve a little turmeric in 15ml/1 tbsp hot water in a small bowl. Stir into half the cooked rice until it is uniformly yellow. Carefully mix the yellow rice into the plain rice.

5 Add the spice and onion paste and fry for about 5 minutes.

6 Return the meat to the pan, together with 300ml/½ pint/1¼ cups water. Cover and simmer for 1–1½ hours or until the meat is tender. Serve with plain and yellow rice, and a raita, if you like.

DHANSAK

About 13 centuries ago, a small group of Persians fled their country to avoid religious persecution and landed in the state of Gujarat. They became known as Parsis and they adopted Gujarati as their language; they developed a Parsi version, which is slightly different from the local form. In native Gujarati, dhan means wealth, but in Parsi Gujarati, it means rice and sak is vegetables. A serving of dhansak is not complete without caramelized basmati rice, the traditional accompaniment.

SERVES 4–6

90ml/6 tbsp vegetable oil
5 fresh green chillies, chopped
2.5cm/1in piece fresh root ginger, grated
3 garlic cloves, crushed, plus 1 garlic
    clove, sliced
2 bay leaves
5cm/2in piece cinnamon stick
900g/2lb lean lamb, cut into large pieces
600ml/1 pint/2½ cups water
175g/6oz/¾ cup red whole lentils, washed
    and drained
50g/2oz/¼ cup each chana dhal or yellow
    split peas, husked moong dhal and red
    lentils, washed and drained
2 potatoes, cut and soaked in water
1 aubergine (eggplant), cut and soaked
    in water
4 onions, finely sliced, deep-fried and
    drained
50g/2oz fresh spinach, trimmed, washed
    and chopped, or 50g/2oz frozen
    spinach, thawed
25g/1oz fenugreek leaves, fresh or dried
115g/4oz carrots, or pumpkin if in season
115g/4oz fresh coriander (cilantro),
    chopped
50g/2oz fresh mint, chopped, or
    15ml/1 tbsp mint sauce
30ml/2 tbsp dhansak masala
30ml/2 tbsp sambhar masala
10ml/2 tsp soft brown sugar
60ml/4 tbsp tamarind juice
salt

VARIATION
Pumpkin is the traditional vegetable used for dhansak. It also helps to tenderize the meat, and will add a fabulous rich golden colour to the dish.

COOK'S TIP
All lentils require gentle cooking over a low to medium heat. They will not soften at high temperatures.

1 Heat 45ml/3 tbsp of the oil in a wok, karahi or large pan, and gently fry the fresh chillies, ginger, crushed garlic, bay leaves and cinnamon for 2 minutes. Add the lamb pieces and the measured water. Bring to the boil then simmer, covered, until the lamb is half cooked.

2 Drain the meat stock into another pan and put the lamb aside. Add the lentils to the stock and cook gently for 25–30 minutes until they are tender. Mash the lentils with the back of a spoon.

3 Drain the potatoes and aubergine and add to the lentils. Reserve a little of the deep-fried onions and stir the remainder into the pan, along with the spinach, fenugreek and carrot or pumpkin.

4 Add some hot water to the pan if the mixture seems too thick. Cook until the vegetables are tender, then mash again with a spoon, keeping the vegetables a little coarse.

5 Heat 15ml/1 tbsp of the vegetable oil in a large frying pan. Reserve a few coriander and mint leaves to use as a garnish, and gently fry the remaining leaves with the dhansak and sambhar masala, salt and sugar. Add the lamb pieces and fry gently for 5 minutes.

6 Add the lamb and spices to the lentils and stir. As lentils absorb fluids, adjust the consistency if necessary. Cover, reduce the heat and cook until the lamb is tender. Mix in the tamarind juice.

7 Heat the remaining vegetable oil in a small pan and fry the sliced garlic clove until golden brown.

8 Sprinkle the fried garlic slices over the dhansak. Garnish with the remaining deep-fried onion and the reserved fresh coriander and mint leaves. Serve the dish hot, with Caramelized Basmati Rice if you like.

PORK BALCHAO

Pork and beef dishes are not very common in India, but Goa, on the west coast of the country, has a cuisine that has been influenced by three religions: Hinduism, Islam and Christianity. Goa was colonized by the Portuguese for nearly four centuries and during this time a Jesuit father, Francis Xavier, brought about a calming influence between the religions. The region became known for its religious tolerance, and this is one tradition that has not faded with the passing of time.

SERVES 4

60ml/4 tbsp vegetable oil
15ml/1 tbsp grated fresh root ginger
15ml/1 tbsp crushed garlic
2.5cm/1in piece cinnamon stick,
  broken up
2–4 dried red chillies, chopped or torn
4 cloves
10ml/2 tsp cumin seeds
10 black peppercorns
675g/1½ lb cubed leg of pork, crackling
  and visible fat removed
5ml/1 tsp ground turmeric
200ml/7fl oz/scant 1 cup warm water
25ml/1½ tbsp tomato purée (paste)
2.5ml/½ tsp chilli powder (optional)
1 large onion, finely sliced
5ml/1 tsp salt
5ml/1 tsp granulated sugar
10ml/2 tbsp cider vinegar

1 Heat 30ml/2 tbsp of the oil in a wok, karahi or large pan, and add the ginger and garlic. Fry for 30 seconds.

2 Grind the next five ingredients to a fine powder, using a spice mill or coffee grinder. Add the spice mix to the pan and fry for a further 30 seconds, stirring.

3 Add the pork and turmeric and increase the heat slightly. Fry for 5–6 minutes or until the meat starts to release its juices, stirring regularly.

4 Add the water, tomato purée, chilli powder, if using, and bring to the boil. Cover the pan and simmer gently for 35–40 minutes.

5 Heat the remaining oil and fry the onion for 8–9 minutes until browned, stirring regularly.

6 Add the fried onion to the pork along with the salt, sugar and vinegar. Stir, cover and simmer for 30–35 minutes or until the pork is tender. Remove from the heat and serve.

COOK'S TIP
Balchao will keep well in the refrigerator for up to 7 days. Before reheating, bring to room temperature. Add a little warm water during reheating, if necessary.

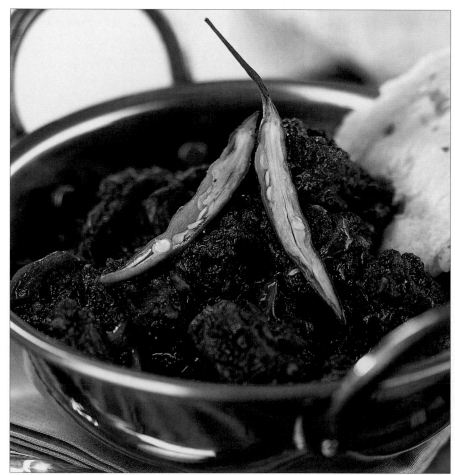

GOAN PRAWN CURRY

The cuisine of Goa is well known for its excellent range of fish and shellfish-based recipes, such as this one for prawns. Numerous varieties of fish and shellfish are found along the extended coastline and the network of inland waterways.

SERVES 4

15g/½oz/1 tbsp ghee or butter
2 garlic cloves, crushed
450g/1lb small raw prawns (shrimp), peeled and deveined
15ml/1 tbsp groundnut (peanut) oil
4 cardamom pods
4 cloves
5cm/2in piece cinnamon stick
15ml/1 tbsp mustard seeds
1 large onion, finely chopped
½–1 fresh red chilli, seeded and sliced
4 tomatoes, peeled, seeded and chopped
175ml/6fl oz/¾ cup fish stock or water
350ml/12fl oz/1½ cups coconut milk
45ml/3 tbsp Fragrant Spice Mix (see Cook's Tip)
10–20ml/2–4 tsp chilli powder
salt
turmeric-coloured basmati rice, to serve

1 Melt the ghee or butter in a wok, karahi or large pan, add the garlic and stir over a low heat for a few seconds. Add the prawns and stir-fry briskly to coat. Transfer to a plate and set aside.

VARIATION
For a reduced fat version, use the same quantity of semi-skimmed (low-fat) milk instead of the coconut milk.

2 In the same pan, heat the oil and fry the cardamom, cloves and cinnamon for 2 minutes. Add the mustard seeds and fry for 1 minute. Add the onion and chilli and fry for 7–8 minutes or until softened and lightly browned.

3 Add the remaining ingredients and bring to a slow simmer. Cook gently for 6–8 minutes and add the prawns. Simmer for 5–8 minutes until the prawns are cooked through. Serve the curry with turmeric-coloured basmati rice.

COOK'S TIP
To make a Fragrant Spice Mix, dry-fry 25ml/1½ tbsp coriander seeds, 15ml/1 tbsp mixed peppercorns, 5ml/1 tsp cumin seeds, 1.5ml/¼ tsp fenugreek seeds and 1.5ml/¼ tsp fennel seeds until aromatic, then grind finely in a spice mill.

PARSI PRAWN CURRY

After landing on the west coast of India, the Parsi community migrated to different parts of the country. The majority, however, made Bombay their home. They have cleverly integrated their cooking style into the exotic tastes of Indian cuisine, as this curry shows.

2 Add the chopped onions to the other ingredients in the pan and fry gently until the chopped onions become translucent, then fold in the tamarind juice, mint sauce, sugar and salt. Simmer for a further 3 minutes.

3 Carefully peel and devein the king prawns, then pat them dry with kitchen paper. Add the prawns to the spice mixture with a small amount of water and stir-fry until the prawns turn bright orange/pink.

SERVES 4–6

60ml/4 tbsp vegetable oil
1 onion, finely sliced, plus 2 onions, finely chopped
6 garlic cloves, crushed
5ml/1 tsp chilli powder
7.5ml/1½ tsp ground turmeric
50ml/2fl oz/¼ cup tamarind juice
5ml/1 tsp mint sauce
15ml/1 tbsp demerara (raw) sugar
450g/1lb raw king prawns (jumbo shrimp)
75g/3oz coriander (cilantro) leaves, chopped, plus extra leaves to garnish
salt

1 Heat the oil and fry the sliced onion. In a bowl, mix the garlic, chilli powder and turmeric with water to form a paste. Add to the onion and cook.

4 When the prawns are cooked, add the coriander leaves and stir-fry on a high heat to thicken the sauce. Garnish with extra coriander leaves and serve.

FISH CAKES

Goan fish and shellfish are skilfully prepared with spices to make cakes of all shapes and sizes, while the rest of India makes fish kababs. Although haddock is used in this recipe, you can use other less expensive white fish, such as coley or whiting.

MAKES 20

450g/1lb skinned haddock or cod
2 potatoes, peeled, boiled and
  coarsely mashed
4 spring onions (scallions),
  finely chopped
4 fresh green chillies, finely chopped
5cm/2in piece fresh root ginger, crushed
a few coriander (cilantro) and mint
  sprigs, chopped
2 eggs
breadcrumbs, for coating
vegetable oil, for shallow frying
salt and ground black pepper
lemon wedges and chilli sauce,
  to serve

1 Place the skinned fish in a lightly greased steamer and steam gently until cooked. Remove the steamer from the hob (stovetop) but leave the fish on the steaming tray until cool.

2 When the fish is cool, crumble it coarsely into a large bowl, using a fork. Mix in the mashed potatoes, spring onions, chillies, crushed ginger, chopped coriander and mint, and one of the eggs. Season to taste with salt and pepper.

COOK'S TIP
For a quick version, used canned tuna in brine and omit step 1. Make sure the tuna is thoroughly drained before use.

3 Shape into cakes. Beat the remaining egg and dip the cakes in it, then coat with the breadcrumbs. Heat the oil and fry the cakes until brown on all sides. Serve as an appetizer or as a side dish, with the lemon wedges and chilli sauce.

SPICY OMELETTE

Another popular contribution by the Parsis, this irresistible omelette is known as poro *in their language. Parsi food originated along the shores of the Caspian Sea, and the cuisine offers some unique flavours, which appeal to both Eastern and Western palates.*

SERVES 4–6

30ml/2 tbsp vegetable oil
1 onion, finely chopped
2.5ml/½ tsp ground cumin
1 garlic clove, crushed
1 or 2 fresh green chillies, finely chopped
a few coriander (cilantro) sprigs,
   chopped, plus extra, to garnish
1 firm tomato, chopped
1 small potato, cubed and boiled
25g/1oz/¼ cup cooked peas
25g/1oz/¼ cup cooked sweetcorn,
   or canned sweetcorn, drained
2 eggs, beaten
25g/1oz/¼ cup grated cheese
salt and ground black pepper

1 Heat the vegetable oil in a wok, karahi or large pan, and fry the next nine ingredients until they are well blended but the potato and tomato are still firm. Season to taste with salt and ground black pepper.

2 Increase the heat and pour in the beaten eggs. Reduce the heat, cover and cook until the bottom layer is brown. Turn the omelette over and sprinkle with the grated cheese. Place under a hot grill (broiler) and cook until the egg sets and the cheese has melted.

3 Garnish the omelette with sprigs of coriander and serve with salad for a light lunch. If you prefer, serve it for breakfast, in the typical Parsi style.

VARIATION
You can use any vegetable with the potatoes. Try thickly sliced button (white) mushrooms, added in step 1.

EGGS BAKED on CHIPSTICKS

This is an unusual and delicious way of combining eggs with potato sticks, and is known as sali pur eeda *in the Parsi language. The potato sticks are cooked with spices to form a pancake. Eggs are then placed on top of the potato pancake and gently cooked.*

SERVES 4–6

225g/8oz salted chipsticks
2 fresh green chillies, finely chopped
a few coriander (cilantro) sprigs, chopped
1.5ml/¼ tsp ground turmeric
60ml/4 tbsp vegetable oil
75ml/5 tbsp water
6 eggs
3 spring onions (scallions), finely chopped
salt and ground black pepper

1 In a bowl, mix the salted chipsticks, chopped chillies, coriander and turmeric. Heat 30ml/2 tbsp of the oil in a heavy frying pan. Add the chipstick mixture and water. Cook until the chipsticks turn soft, and then crisp.

2 Place a dinner plate over the frying pan, and hold in place as you turn the pan over and carefully transfer the chipstick pancake on to the plate. Heat the remaining oil in the pan and slide the pancake back into the frying pan to brown the other side.

3 Gently break the eggs over the pancake, cover the frying pan and allow the eggs to set over a low heat. Season well and sprinkle with spring onions. Cook until the base is crisp. Serve hot for breakfast in the Parsi style, or with chapatis and a salad for lunch or supper.

STUFFED OKRA

The Gujarati community excels in the art of vegetarian cooking. Although some meat-and poultry-based dishes originated in Gujarat due to the presence of the Parsis, the native Gujaratis are strict vegetarians, who do not even eat eggs. Stuffed okra is easy to make and will happily accompany most meat and poultry dishes.

SERVES 4–6

225g/8oz large okra
15ml/1 tbsp amchur (dry
    mango powder)
2.5ml/½ tsp ground ginger
2.5ml/½ tsp ground cumin
2.5ml/½ tsp chilli powder
    (optional)
2.5ml/½ tsp ground turmeric
vegetable oil, for frying and mixing
30ml/2 tbsp cornflour (cornstarch),
    placed in a plastic bag
salt

1 Wash the okra and trim the tips. Make a slit lengthwise in the centre of each okra; do not cut all the way through.

2 In a bowl, mix the amchur, ginger, cumin, chilli, if using, turmeric and salt with a few drops of vegetable oil. Leave the mixture to rest for 1–2 hours or refrigerate overnight.

3 Using your fingers, part the slit of each okra carefully without opening it all the way and fill each with as much filling as possible. Put all the okra into the plastic bag with the cornflour and shake the bag carefully to cover the okra evenly.

4 Fill a wok, karahi or large pan with enough oil to sit 2.5cm/1in deep. Heat the oil and fry the okra in small batches for 5–8 minutes or until they are brown and slightly crisp. Serve hot with any meat, poultry or fish curry.

COOK'S TIP
When buying okra, choose one without any blemishes. Wash them thoroughly, rubbing each one gently with a soft vegetable brush or your fingertips.

OKRA in YOGURT

This tangy vegetable dish can be served as an accompaniment, but also makes an excellent vegetarian meal served with tarka dhal and chapatis. The secret of cooking okra is not to disturb its glutinous tendencies by overcooking, as the results can be unpleasant. Do follow the temperature and timing carefully.

SERVES 4

450g/1lb okra
30ml/2 tbsp vegetable oil
2.5ml/½ tsp onion seeds
3 fresh red or green chillies, chopped
1 onion, sliced
1.5ml/¼ tsp ground turmeric
10ml/2 tsp desiccated (dry, unsweetened, shredded) coconut
2.5ml/½ tsp salt
15ml/1 tbsp natural (plain) yogurt
2 tomatoes, quartered
15ml/1 tbsp chopped fresh coriander (cilantro)

1 Wash and trim the okra, cut into 1cm/½in pieces and set aside.

2 Heat the oil in a wok, karahi or large pan. Add the onion seeds, green chillies and onion, and fry for 5 minutes.

3 When the onion is golden brown, lower the heat and add the turmeric, desiccated coconut and salt. Fry for about 1 minute, stirring all the time.

4 Add the okra pieces to the pan. Turn the heat to medium-high and stir-fry briskly for a few minutes, until the okra has turned lightly golden.

5 Add the yogurt, tomatoes and fresh coriander. Cook for a further 2 minutes. Transfer to a warmed serving dish and serve immediately, as a side dish.

BOMBAY POTATO

This well-known dish is served in most Indian restaurants in the West, but it does not exist in Mumbai, formerly Bombay. The origin of the name Bombay potato remains a mystery, although one theory is that it resembles a dish sold by street vendors there.

SERVES 4–6

450g/1lb whole new potatoes
5ml/1 tsp ground turmeric
60ml/4 tbsp vegetable oil
2 dried red chillies
6–8 curry leaves
2 onions, finely chopped
2 fresh green chillies, finely chopped
50g/2oz coarsely chopped fresh coriander
  (cilantro)
1.5ml/¼ tsp asafoetida
2.5ml/½ tsp each cumin, mustard,
  onion, fennel and nigella seeds
lemon juice, to taste
salt

1 Scrub the potatoes under running water and cut into small pieces. Boil the potatoes in water with a little salt and 2.5ml/½ tsp of the turmeric until tender. Drain well then coarsely mash. Set aside.

2 Heat the oil and fry the dried chillies and curry leaves until the chillies are nearly burnt. Add the onions, green chillies, coriander, remaining turmeric, asafoetida and spice seeds and cook until the onions are soft.

3 Fold in the potatoes and add a few drops of water. Cook gently over a low heat for 10 minutes, mixing well to ensure even distribution of the spices. Add lemon juice to taste.

4 Serve the potatoes with parathas or, as they would be eaten in Bombay, as a snack with soft white bread rolls.

CHICKPEAS with SPICED POTATO CAKES

This is a typical Bombay street snack; the kind that the Bombayites would happily eat while walking along the beach or watching a cricket match. It is the kind of food that brings together the cosmopolitan population of the city.

MAKES 10–12

30ml/2 tbsp vegetable oil
30ml/2 tbsp ground coriander
30ml/2 tbsp ground cumin
2.5ml/½ tsp ground turmeric
2.5ml/½ tsp salt
2.5ml/½ tsp granulated sugar
30ml/2 tbsp gram flour (besan), mixed
　　with a little water to make a paste
450g/1lb/3 cups boiled chickpeas, drained
2 fresh green chillies, chopped
5cm/2in piece fresh root ginger, crushed
85g/3oz chopped fresh coriander
　　(cilantro)
2 firm tomatoes, chopped
fresh mint sprigs, to garnish

For the potato cakes
450g/1lb potatoes, boiled and mashed
4 fresh green chillies, finely chopped
50g/2oz finely chopped fresh coriander
　　(cilantro)
7.5ml/1½ tsp ground cumin
5ml/1 tsp amchur (dry mango powder)
vegetable oil, for shallow frying
salt

1 To prepare the chickpeas, heat the oil in a wok, karahi or large pan. Fry the coriander, cumin, turmeric, salt, sugar and gram flour paste until the water has evaporated and the oil has separated.

2 Add the chickpeas to the spices in the pan, and stir in the chopped chillies, ginger, fresh coriander and tomatoes. Toss the ingredients well and simmer gently for about 5 minutes. Transfer to a serving dish and keep warm.

3 To make the potato cakes, place the mashed potato in a large bowl and add the green chillies, chopped fresh coriander, cumin and amchur powder and salt. Mix together until all the ingredients are well blended.

4 Using your hands, shape the potato mixture into little cakes. Heat the oil in a shallow frying pan and fry the cakes on both sides until golden brown. Transfer to a serving dish, garnish with mint sprigs and serve with the chickpeas.

POTATOES in a YOGURT SAUCE

The potato was first introduced to India by Dutch traders, and it has since been elevated to gourmet status. In Indian cuisine, the humble potato takes on delicious flavourings of simple whole spices, or of blends of spices ground together.

SERVES 4

12 new potatoes, halved
300ml/½ pint/1¼ cups natural (plain) yogurt, whisked
300ml/½ pint/1¼ cups water
1.5ml/¼ tsp ground turmeric
5ml/1 tsp chilli powder
5ml/1 tsp ground coriander
2.5ml/½ tsp ground cumin
5ml/1 tsp salt
5ml/1 tsp soft brown sugar
30ml/2 tbsp vegetable oil
5ml/1 tsp cumin seeds
15ml/1 tbsp chopped fresh coriander (cilantro), plus extra sprigs to garnish (optional)
2 fresh green chillies, sliced

1 Boil the halved new potatoes with their skins on in a large pan of salted water, until they are just tender. Drain the potatoes and set aside.

2 Mix together the natural yogurt, water, turmeric, chilli powder, ground coriander, ground cumin, salt and sugar in a bowl. Set the mixture aside.

COOK'S TIPS

• If new potatoes are out of season and unavailable, you could use 450g/1lb ordinary potatoes instead. Peel and wash them and cut into large chunks, then cook as described above.
• Add 10ml/2 tsp gram flour (besan) to the yogurt to prevent it curdling.

3 Heat the vegetable oil in a wok, karahi or large pan, and add the cumin seeds. Fry gently until they begin to splutter.

4 Reduce the heat, stir in the yogurt mixture and cook for about 3 minutes over a medium heat.

5 Add the chopped fresh coriander, green chillies and cooked potatoes. Blend everything together and cook for a further 5–7 minutes, stirring the mixture occasionally.

6 Transfer to a warmed serving dish and garnish with the coriander sprig, if you like. This dish goes very well with hot bhaturas or chapatis.

STUFFED VEGETABLES

It is hard to beat the Gujarati community when it comes to the creation of imaginative vegetarian dishes. In this fabulous recipe, two different vegetables are stuffed with an irresistible blend of spices and peanuts.

SERVES 4

12 small potatoes
8 baby aubergines (eggplant)
single (light) cream, to garnish

For the stuffing
15ml/1 tbsp sesame seeds
30ml/2 tbsp ground coriander
30ml/2 tbsp ground cumin
2.5ml/½ tsp salt
1.5ml/¼ tsp chilli powder
2.5ml/½ tsp ground turmeric
10ml/2 tsp granulated sugar
1.5ml/¼ tsp garam masala
15ml/1 tbsp peanuts, roughly crushed
15ml/1 tbsp gram flour (besan)
2 garlic cloves, crushed
15ml/1 tbsp lemon juice
30ml/2 tbsp chopped fresh coriander
   (cilantro)

For the sauce
30ml/2 tbsp vegetable oil
2.5ml/½ tsp black mustard seeds
400g/14oz can chopped tomatoes
30ml/2 tbsp chopped fresh coriander
   (cilantro)
150ml/¼ pint/⅔ cup water

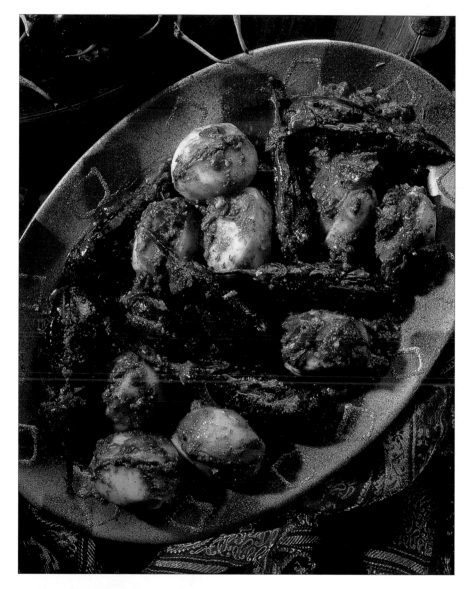

1 Preheat the oven to 200°C/400°F/
Gas 6. Make slits in the potatoes and
baby aubergines, making sure that you
do not cut right through.

2 Mix all the ingredients for the stuffing
together on a plate.

3 Carefully stuff the potatoes and
aubergines with the spice mixture.

4 Place the potatoes and aubergines in
a greased ovenproof dish.

5 Heat the oil in a pan and fry the
mustard seeds for 2 minutes until they
begin to splutter, then add the tomatoes,
coriander and any leftover stuffing,
together with the water. Simmer for
5 minutes until the sauce thickens.

6 Pour the sauce over the potatoes
and aubergines. Cover and bake for
25–30 minutes until the vegetables are
soft. Garnish with single cream, if using.
Serve with any Indian bread or with a
meat or chicken curry of your choice.

RICES AND BREADS

An Indian meal is always served with rice or bread. Basmati rice, with its distinctive aromatic flavour, is the most popular variety. Leavened breads, such as naan, are widely eaten in the north and west, while flat, unleavened chapatis and parathas are the breads of the south.

SAFFRON RICE

The saffron crocus is a perennial bulb that only flowers for two weeks of the year, and each stigma has to be removed by hand and dried with care. Consequently, saffron is said to be worth its weight in gold. Kashmir in the northern region of India and La Manche in Spain are the world's two major producers of saffron. In Indian cooking, saffron is used as a colorant in both sweet and savoury dishes.

SERVES 6

450g/1lb/2⅓ cups basmati rice, soaked
    for 20–30 minutes
750ml/1¼ pints/3 cups water
3 green cardamom pods
2 cloves
5ml/1 tsp salt
45ml/3 tbsp semi-skimmed (low-fat) milk
2.5ml/½ tsp saffron threads, crushed

COOK'S TIP
The saffron milk can be heated in the microwave. Mix the milk and saffron threads in a suitable container and warm them for 1 minute on Low.

1 Drain the basmati rice and place in a large pan. Pour in the water. Add the cardamoms, cloves and salt. Stir, then bring to the boil. Lower the heat and cover tightly, and simmer for 5 minutes.

2 Meanwhile, place the milk in a small pan. Add the saffron threads and heat through gently.

3 Add the saffron milk to the rice and stir. Cover again and continue cooking over a low heat for 5–6 minutes.

4 Remove the pan from the heat without lifting the lid. Leave the rice to stand for about 5 minutes, then fork through just before serving.

COOK'S TIP
Wash the rice in cold water before soaking for longer, fluffier cooked rice.

CARAMELIZED BASMATI RICE

This is the traditional accompaniment to a dhansak *curry. Sugar is caramelized in hot oil before the rice is added, along with a few whole spices.*

SERVES 4

225g/8oz/generous 1 cup basmati rice,
    washed and soaked for 20–30 minutes
45ml/3 tbsp vegetable oil
20ml/4 tsp granulated sugar
4–5 green cardamom pods, bruised
2.5cm/1in piece cinnamon stick
4 cloves
1 bay leaf, crumpled
½ tsp salt
475ml/16fl oz/2 cups hot water

1 Put the basmati rice in a colander and leave to drain.

2 In a large pan, heat the vegetable oil over a medium heat. When the oil is hot, add the granulated sugar and wait until it is caramelized.

3 Reduce the heat to low and add the spices and bay leaf. Let sizzle for about 15–20 seconds, then add the rice and salt. Fry gently, stirring, for 2–3 minutes.

4 Pour in the water and bring to the boil. Let it boil steadily for 2 minutes then reduce the heat to very low. Cover the pan and cook for 8 minutes.

5 Remove the rice from the heat and let it stand for 6–8 minutes. Gently fluff up the rice with a fork and transfer to a warmed dish to serve.

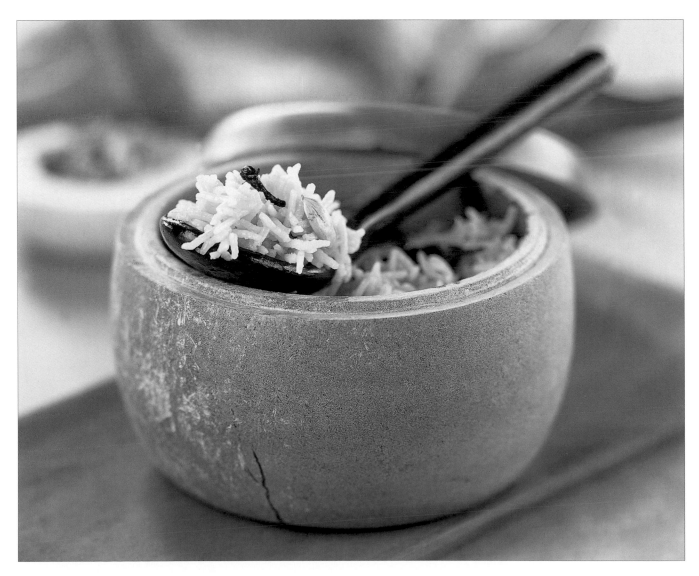

CLASSIC PULAO

The exquisite flavour of basmati rice flavoured with stock and the heady aroma of saffron is the classic character of a traditional pulao. The secret of a perfect pulao is to wash the rice thoroughly, then soak it briefly. Soaking before cooking softens and moistens the grains, enabling the rice to absorb moisture during cooking, and resulting in fluffier rice.

SERVES 4

600ml/1 pint/2½ cups hot chicken
  stock
generous pinch of saffron threads
50g/2oz/¼ cup butter
1 onion, chopped
1 garlic clove, crushed
2.5cm/1in piece cinnamon stick
6 green cardamom pods
1 bay leaf
250g/9oz/1⅓ cups basmati rice, soaked
  for 20–30 minutes
50g/2oz/⅓ cup sultanas (golden raisins)
15ml/1 tbsp vegetable oil
50g/2oz/½ cup cashew nuts
naan bread and Tomato and Onion
  Salad, to serve

3 Drain the rice and add to the pan, then cook, stirring, for 2 minutes more. Pour in the saffron stock and add the sultanas. Bring to the boil, stir, then lower the heat, cover and cook gently for 10 minutes or until the rice is tender and the liquid has all been absorbed.

4 Meanwhile, heat the oil in a wok, karahi or large pan and fry the cashew nuts until browned. Drain on kitchen paper, then sprinkle the cashew nuts over the rice. Serve with naan bread and Tomato and Onion Salad, or with Mughlai-style Leg of Lamb.

1 Pour the hot chicken stock into a jug (pitcher). Stir in the saffron threads and set aside.

2 Heat the butter in a pan and fry the onion and garlic for 5 minutes. Stir in the cinnamon stick, cardamoms and bay leaf and cook for 2 minutes.

NUT PULAO

Known as pilau in Persia, pilaff in Turkey and pulao in India, these rice dishes are always made with the best-quality long grain rice. In India, basmati rice is the natural choice. There are different variations of this recipe, and this one, with walnuts and cashews, makes an ideal dish for vegetarians when served with a raita or natural yogurt.

SERVES 4

15–30ml/1–2 tbsp vegetable oil
1 onion, chopped
1 garlic clove, crushed
1 large carrot, coarsely grated
225g/8oz/generous 1 cup basmati rice,
    soaked for 20–30 minutes
5ml/1 tsp cumin seeds
10ml/2 tsp ground coriander
10ml/2 tsp black mustard seeds (optional)
4 green cardamom pods
450ml/¾ pint/scant 2 cups vegetable stock
1 bay leaf
75g/3oz/¾ cup unsalted walnuts and
    cashew nuts
salt and ground black pepper
fresh coriander (cilantro) sprigs, to garnish

1 Heat the oil in a wok, karahi or large pan. Fry the onion, garlic and carrot for 3–4 minutes. Drain the rice and add to the spices. Cook for 2 minutes, stirring to coat the grains in oil.

2 Pour in the vegetable stock, stirring. Add the bay leaf and season well.

3 Bring to the boil, lower the heat, cover and simmer very gently for 10–12 minutes.

4 Remove the pan from the heat without lifting the lid. Leave to stand for 5 minutes, then check the rice. If it is cooked, there will be small steam holes on the surface of the rice. Discard the bay leaf and the cardamom pods.

COOK'S TIP
Use a metal slotted spoon or a fork while stirring in the nuts. Wooden spoons will squash the delicate rice grains.

5 Stir in the walnuts and cashew nuts and check the seasoning. Spoon on to a warmed platter, garnish with the fresh coriander and serve.

PULAO in AROMATIC LAMB STOCK

A typical north Indian dish known as yakhni pulao, *this is rich and highly aromatic. Traditionally, lamb is cooked on the bone, which adds extra flavour to the stock. If you buy a leg of lamb and bone it yourself, do save the bones and add them to the stock at step 1; they can be discarded later in the recipe.*

SERVES 4–6

900g/2lb chicken pieces or lean lamb, cubed
600ml/1 pint/2½ cups water
4 green cardamom pods
2 black cardamom pods
10 whole peppercorns
4 cloves
1 onion, sliced
450g/1lb/2⅓ cups basmati rice, washed
   and drained
8–10 saffron threads
2 garlic cloves, crushed
5cm/2in piece fresh root ginger, crushed
5cm/2in piece cinnamon stick
salt
175g/6oz/generous 1 cup sultanas
   (golden raisins) and almonds, sautéed,
   to garnish

1 Place the chicken pieces or cubed lamb in a large pan with the water, cardamoms, peppercorns, cloves and sliced onion. Add salt to taste, and cook until the meat is tender. Remove the meat with a slotted spoon and keep warm. Strain the stock, if you wish, and return it to the pan.

2 Add the drained rice, saffron, garlic, ginger and cinnamon to the stock in the pan and bring the contents to the boil.

3 Quickly add the meat and stir well. Bring the stock back to the boil, reduce the heat and cover. Cook for about 15–20 minutes.

4 Remove from the heat and stand for 5 minutes. Transfer the contents of the pan to a warmed serving platter and garnish with the sultanas and sautéed almonds before serving.

COOK'S TIP
When washing rice, toss and turn it very gently to avoid damage to the delicate grains of basmati.

CHICKEN PULAO

Like biryanis, pulaos cooked with meat and poultry make a convenient one-pot meal.
A vegetable curry makes a good accompaniment, although for a simpler meal, such as
supper, you could serve the pulao with a simple raita, combining natural yogurt with
any raw vegetable, such as white cabbage, grated carrots, or cauliflower florets.

SERVES 4

400g/14oz/2 cups basmati rice
75g/3oz/6 tbsp ghee or unsalted
  (sweet) butter
1 onion, sliced
1.5ml/¼ tsp mixed onion and mustard
  seeds
3 curry leaves
5ml/1 tsp grated fresh root ginger
5ml/1 tsp crushed garlic
5ml/1 tsp ground coriander
5ml/1 tsp chilli powder
7.5ml/1½ tsp salt
2 tomatoes, sliced
1 potato, cubed
50g/2oz/½ cup frozen peas, thawed
175g/6oz chicken breast fillets, skinned
  and cubed
60ml/4 tbsp chopped fresh coriander
  (cilantro)
2 fresh green chillies, chopped
700ml/1¼ pints/3 cups water

1 Wash the rice thoroughly under running water, then leave to soak for 30 minutes. Drain and set aside in a sieve (strainer).

2 In a pan, melt the ghee or butter and fry the sliced onion until golden.

3 Add the onion and mustard seeds, the curry leaves, ginger, garlic, ground coriander, chilli powder and salt. Stir-fry for about 2 minutes over a low heat: ground spices require only gentle warmth to release their flavours.

4 Add the sliced tomatoes, cubed potato, peas and chicken and mix everything together well.

5 Add the rice and stir gently to combine with the other ingredients.

6 Add the coriander and chillies. Mix and stir-fry for 1 minute. Pour in the water, bring to the boil and then lower the heat. Cover and cook for 20 minutes. Remove from the heat and leave the pulao to stand for 6–8 minutes. Serve.

TRICOLOUR PULAO

Most Indian restaurants in the West serve this popular vegetable pulao, which has three different vegetables. The effect is easily achieved with canned or frozen vegetables, but for entertaining or a special occasion dinner, you may prefer to use fresh produce.

SERVES 4–6

225g/8oz/1 cup basmati rice, rinsed
   and soaked for 30 minutes
30ml/2 tbsp vegetable oil
2.5ml/½ tsp cumin seeds
2 dried bay leaves
4 green cardamom pods
4 cloves
1 onion, finely chopped
1 carrot, finely diced
50g/2oz/½ cup frozen peas, thawed
50g/2oz/⅓ cup frozen sweetcorn, thawed
25g/1oz/¼ cup cashew nuts, lightly fried
475ml/16fl oz/2 cups water
1.5ml/¼ tsp ground cumin
salt

1 Heat the oil in a wok, karahi or large pan over a medium heat, and fry the cumin seeds for 2 minutes. Add the bay leaves, cardamoms and cloves, and fry gently for 2 minutes more, stirring the spices from time to time.

2 Add the onion and fry until lightly browned. Stir in the diced carrot and cook, stirring, for 3–4 minutes.

3 Drain the soaked basmati rice and add to the contents in the pan. Stir well to mix. Add the peas, sweetcorn and fried cashew nuts.

4 Add the measured water and the remaining spices, and add salt to taste. Bring to the boil, cover and simmer for 15 minutes over a low heat until all the water is absorbed.

5 Leave to stand, covered, for 10 minutes. Transfer to a warmed dish and serve.

PRAWN BIRYANI

The recipe for biryani originated with mutton, but its popularity has tempted Indian chefs to create versions using other ingredients. As with all biryanis, this one using prawns is a meal in itself. The classic accompaniment to any biryani is a raita.

SERVES 4–6

2 large onions, finely sliced and
    deep-fried
300ml/½ pint/1¼ cups natural
    (plain) yogurt
30ml/2 tbsp tomato purée (paste)
60ml/4 tbsp green masala paste
30ml/2 tbsp lemon juice
5ml/1 tsp black cumin seeds
5cm/2in piece cinnamon stick, or
    1.5ml/¼ tsp ground cinnamon
4 green cardamom pods
450g/1lb raw king prawns (jumbo
    shrimp), peeled and deveined
225g/8oz/3 cups small whole button
    (white) mushrooms
225g/8oz/2 cups frozen peas, thawed
450g/1lb/2⅓ cups basmati rice,
    soaked for 5 minutes in boiled
    water and drained
300ml/½ pint/1¼ cups water
1 sachet saffron powder, mixed in
    90ml/6 tbsp milk
30ml/2 tbsp ghee or unsalted (sweet)
    butter
salt

1 In a bowl, mix the onions, yogurt, tomato purée, masala paste, lemon juice, cumin seeds, cinnamon and cardamom, with salt to taste. Fold in the prawns, mushrooms and peas. Leave for 2 hours. Preheat the oven to 190°C/375°F/Gas 5.

2 Grease the base of a heavy pan and add the prawns, vegetables and any marinade juices. Cover with the drained rice and smooth the surface gently until you have an even layer.

3 Pour the water over the surface of the rice. Make holes through the rice with the handle of a spoon and pour into each a little saffron milk. Place knobs (pats) of ghee or butter on the surface.

4 Place a circular piece of foil on top of the rice. Cover and cook in the oven for 45–50 minutes. Allow to stand for 8–10 minutes, then stir the biryani and serve hot.

TOMATO and SPINACH PULAO

A tasty and nourishing dish for vegetarians and meat eaters alike. Serve it with another vegetable curry, or with tandoori chicken, marinated fried fish or shammi kabab. Add a cooling fruit raita for a completely balanced meal.

2 Drain the rice, add it to the pan and cook for a further 1–2 minutes, stirring, until the rice is coated.

3 Stir in the dhana jeera powder or coriander and cumin, then add the carrots. Season with salt and pepper. Pour in the stock and stir well to mix.

SERVES 4

30ml/2 tbsp vegetable oil
15ml/1 tbsp ghee or unsalted (sweet) butter
1 onion, chopped
2 garlic cloves, crushed
3 tomatoes, peeled, seeded and chopped
225g/8oz/generous 1 cup brown basmati rice, soaked
10ml/2 tsp dhana jeera powder or 5ml/1 tsp ground coriander and 5ml/1 tsp ground cumin
2 carrots, coarsely grated
900ml/1½ pints/3¾ cups vegetable stock
275g/10oz young spinach leaves
50g/2oz/½ cup unsalted cashew nuts, toasted
salt and ground black pepper
naan bread, to serve

1 Heat the oil and ghee or butter in a wok, karahi or large pan, and fry the onion and garlic for 4–5 minutes until soft. Add the tomatoes and cook for 3–4 minutes, stirring, until thickened.

COOK'S TIP
Leaving to rest for 6–8 minutes before serving makes the rice dry and fluffy.

4 Bring to the boil, then cover tightly and simmer over a very gentle heat for 20–25 minutes, until the rice is tender. Lay the spinach on the surface of the rice, cover again, and cook for a further 2–3 minutes, until the spinach has wilted. Fold the spinach into the rest of the rice and check the seasoning. Sprinkle with toasted cashews and serve with naan.

CHICKEN BIRYANI

Biryani is a meal in itself and needs no accompaniment, except for a raita and some grilled or fried poppadums. It is a dish that is equally at home on the family dining table or as a dinner-party centrepiece.

SERVES 4

10 whole green cardamom pods
275g/10oz/1½ cups basmati rice, soaked
    and drained
2.5ml/½ tsp salt
2–3 whole cloves
5cm/2in piece cinnamon stick
45ml/3 tbsp vegetable oil
3 onions, sliced
4 chicken breast fillets, each about 175g/
    6oz, skinned and cubed
1.5ml/¼ tsp ground cloves
1.5ml/¼ tsp hot chilli powder
5ml/1 tsp ground cumin
5ml/1 tsp ground coriander
2.5ml/½ tsp ground black pepper
3 garlic cloves, chopped
5ml/1 tsp finely chopped fresh root ginger
juice of 1 lemon
4 tomatoes, sliced
30ml/2 tbsp chopped fresh coriander
    (cilantro)
150ml/¼ pint/⅔ cup natural (plain) yogurt,
    plus extra to serve
4–5 saffron threads, soaked in 10ml/2 tsp
    warm milk
150ml/¼ pint/⅔ cup water
toasted flaked (sliced) almonds and fresh
    coriander (cilantro) sprigs, to garnish

1 Preheat the oven to 190°C/375°F/ Gas 5. Remove the seeds from half the cardamom pods and grind them finely, using a pestle and mortar. Set aside the ground seeds.

2 Bring a pan of water to the boil and add the rice, salt, whole cardamom pods, cloves and cinnamon stick. Boil for 2 minutes, then drain, leaving the whole spices in the rice. Keep the rice hot in a covered pan.

3 Heat the oil in a wok, karahi or large pan, and fry the onions for 8 minutes, until softened and browned. Add the chicken and the ground spices, including the ground cardamom seeds. Mix well, then add the garlic, ginger and lemon juice. Stir-fry for about 5 minutes.

4 Transfer the chicken mixture to a casserole and arrange the tomatoes on top. Sprinkle on the fresh coriander, spoon the yogurt evenly on top and cover with the drained rice.

5 Drizzle the saffron milk over the rice and pour over the water. Cover, then bake for 1 hour. Transfer to a serving platter and discard the whole spices. Garnish and serve immediately.

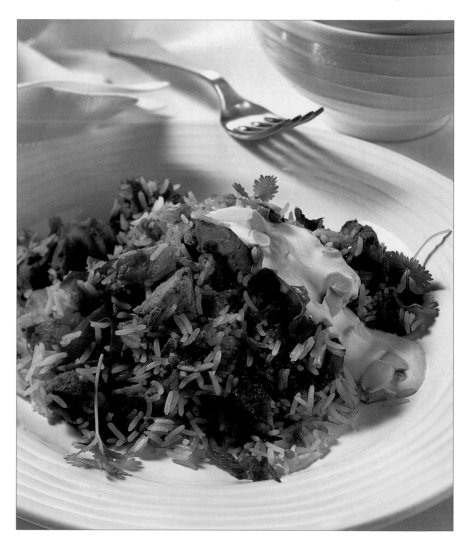

BEEF BIRYANI

This biryani, which uses beef, is a speciality of the Muslim community. The recipe may seem long, but biryani is one of the easiest and most relaxing ways of cooking, especially when you are entertaining. Once the dish is assembled and placed in the oven, it looks after itself and you can happily get on with other things.

SERVES 4

2 large onions
2 garlic cloves, chopped
2.5cm/1in piece of fresh root ginger,
　peeled and roughly chopped
½–1 fresh green chilli, seeded and chopped
small bunch of fresh coriander (cilantro)
60ml/4 tbsp flaked (sliced) almonds
30–45ml/2–3 tbsp water
15ml/1 tbsp ghee or butter, plus
　25g/1oz/2 tbsp butter for the rice
45ml/3 tbsp vegetable oil
30ml/2 tbsp sultanas (golden raisins)
500g/1¼lb braising or stewing steak,
　cubed
5ml/1 tsp ground coriander
15ml/1 tbsp ground cumin
2.5ml/½ tsp ground turmeric
2.5ml/½ tsp ground fenugreek
good pinch of ground cinnamon
175ml/6fl oz/¾ cup natural (plain)
　yogurt, whisked
275g/10oz/1½ cups basmati rice
about 1.2 litres/2 pints/5 cups hot
　chicken stock or water
salt and ground black pepper
2 hard-boiled (hard-cooked) eggs,
　quartered, to garnish
chapatis, to serve

1 Roughly chop one onion and place it in a food processor or blender. Add the garlic, ginger, chilli, fresh coriander and half the flaked almonds. Pour in the water and process to a smooth paste. Transfer the paste to a small bowl and set aside.

2 Finely slice the remaining onion into rings or half rings. Heat half the ghee or butter with half the oil in a heavy flameproof casserole and fry the onion rings for 10–15 minutes until they are a deep golden brown. Transfer to a plate with a slotted spoon. Fry the remaining flaked almonds briefly until golden and set aside with the onion rings, then quickly fry the sultanas until they swell. Transfer to the plate.

3 Heat the remaining ghee or butter in the casserole with a further 15ml/ 1 tbsp of the oil. Fry the cubed meat, in batches, until evenly browned on all sides. Transfer the meat to a plate and set aside.

4 Wipe the casserole clean with kitchen paper, heat the remaining oil and pour in the onion, spice and coriander paste made earlier. Cook over a medium heat for 2–3 minutes, stirring all the time, until the mixture begins to brown lightly. Stir in all the additional spices, season with salt and ground black pepper and cook for 1 minute more.

5 Lower the heat, then stir in the yogurt, a little at a time. When all of it has been incorporated into the spice mixture, return the meat to the casserole. Stir to coat, cover tightly and simmer over a gentle heat for 40–45 minutes until the meat is tender. Meanwhile, soak the rice in a bowl of cold water for 15–20 minutes.

6 Preheat the oven to 160°C/325°F/ Gas 3. Drain the rice, place in a pan and add the hot chicken stock or water, together with a little salt. Bring back to the boil, cover and cook for 5 minutes.

7 Drain the rice, and pile it in a mound on top of the meat in the casserole. Using the handle of a spoon, make a hole through the rice and meat mixture, to the bottom of the pan. Place the fried onions, almonds and sultanas over the top and dot with butter. Cover the casserole tightly with a double layer of foil and secure with a lid.

8 Cook the biryani in the preheated oven for 30–40 minutes. To serve, spoon the mixture on to a warmed serving platter and garnish with the quartered hard-boiled eggs. Serve with chapatis.

COOK'S TIP
Place a piece of buttered greaseproof (waxed) paper on the rice. This will help to keep the top layer moist in the oven.

CHAPATIS

A chapati is an unleavened bread made from chapati flour, a ground wholemeal flour known as atta, which is finer than the Western equivalent. An equal quantity of standard wholemeal flour and plain flour will also produce satisfactory results, although chapati flour is available from Indian grocers. This is the everyday bread of the Indian home.

MAKES 8–10

225g/8oz/2 cups chapati flour or ground
    wholemeal (whole-wheat) flour
2.5ml/½ tsp salt
175ml/6fl oz/¾ cup water

1 Place the flour and salt in a mixing bowl. Make a well in the middle and gradually stir in the water, mixing well with your fingers. Form a supple dough and knead for 7–10 minutes. Ideally, cover with clear film and leave on one side for 15–20 minutes to rest.

2 Divide the dough into 8–10 equal portions. Roll out each piece in a circle on a well-floured surface.

3 Place a *tava* (chapati griddle) or heavy frying pan over a high heat. When steam rises from it, lower the heat to medium and add the first chapati to the pan.

4 When the chapati begins to bubble, turn it over. Press down with a clean dish towel or a flat spoon and turn once again. Remove the cooked chapati from the pan and keep warm in a piece of foil lined with kitchen paper while you cook the other chapatis. Repeat the process until all the breads are cooked. Serve the chapatis immediately.

NAAN

This bread was introduced to India by the Moguls who originally came from Persia via Afghanistan. In Persian, the word naan *means bread. Traditionally, naan is not rolled, but patted and stretched until the teardrop shape is achieved. You can, of course, roll it out to a circle, then gently pull the lower end, which will give you the traditional shape.*

MAKES ABOUT 3

225g/8oz/2 cups unbleached white
    bread flour
2.5ml/1/2 tsp salt
15g/1/2oz fresh yeast
60ml/4 tbsp lukewarm milk
15ml/1 tbsp vegetable oil
30ml/2 tbsp natural (plain) yogurt
1 egg
30–45ml/2–3 tbsp melted ghee or butter,
    for brushing

1 Sift the flour and salt together into a large bowl. In a smaller bowl, cream the yeast with the milk. Set aside for 15 minutes.

2 Add the yeast mixture, oil, yogurt and egg to the flour and mix to a soft dough.

VARIATION

Onion seeds or chopped fresh coriander (cilantro) may also be used as a topping. You could also make wholemeal (whole-wheat) naan by substituting wholemeal flour for some or all of the white flour.

3 Turn the dough out on to a lightly floured surface and knead for about 10 minutes, or until smooth. Return the dough to the bowl, cover and leave in a warm place for about 1 hour, until it has doubled in size. Preheat the oven to its highest setting, at least 230°C/450°F/Gas 8.

4 Turn out the dough back on to the floured surface and knead for a further 2 minutes.

5 Divide into three equal pieces, shape into balls and roll each out into a teardrop shape about 25cm/10in long, 13cm/5in wide and 5mm–8mm/1/4–1/3in thick.

6 Preheat the grill (broiler) to its highest setting. Meanwhile, place the naan on preheated baking sheets and bake for 3–4 minutes, or until puffed up.

7 Remove the naan from the oven and place under the hot grill for a few seconds until the tops brown slightly. Brush with ghee or butter and serve warm.

RED LENTIL PANCAKES

This is a type of dosa, which is essentially a pancake from southern India, but used in the similar fashion to north Indian bread. North Indian breads are made of wholemeal or refined flour; in the south they are made of ground lentils and rice.

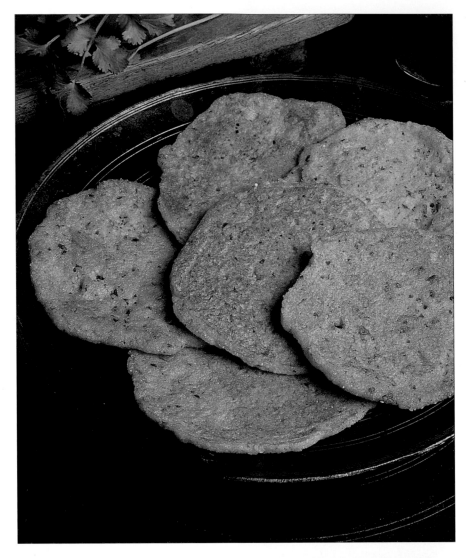

2 Drain off the water and reserve. Place the rice and lentils in a food processor and blend until smooth. Blend in the reserved water.

3 Scrape into a bowl, cover with clear film (plastic wrap) and leave in a warm place to ferment for about 24 hours.

4 Stir in the salt, turmeric, pepper and coriander. Heat a heavy frying pan over a medium heat for a few minutes until hot. Smear with oil and add about 30–45ml/2–3 tbsp batter.

5 Using the rounded base of a soup spoon, gently spread the batter out, using a circular motion, to make a pancake that is 15cm/6in in diameter.

6 Cook in the pan for 1½–2 minutes, or until set. Drizzle a little oil over the pancake and around the edges. Turn over and cook for about 1 minute, or until golden brown. Keep the cooked pancakes warm in a low oven on a heatproof plate placed over simmering water while cooking the remaining pancakes. Serve warm.

MAKES 6 PANCAKES

150g/5oz/¾ cup long grain rice
50g/2oz/¼ cup red lentils
250ml/8fl oz/1 cup warm water
5ml/1 tsp salt
2.5ml/½ tsp ground turmeric
2.5ml/½ tsp ground black pepper
30ml/2 tbsp chopped fresh coriander
　(cilantro)
oil, for frying and drizzling

VARIATION
Add 60ml/4 tbsp grated coconut to the batter just before cooking.

1 Place the long grain rice and lentils in a large mixing bowl, cover with the warm water, and set aside to soak for at least 8 hours or overnight.

PARATHAS

Making a paratha is somewhat similar to the technique used when making flaky pastry.
The difference lies in the handling of the dough; this can be handled freely, unlike that for
a flaky pastry. Parathas are rich in saturated fat, so reserve for special occasions.

MAKES 12–15

350g/12oz/3 cups chapati flour or ground
    wholemeal (whole-wheat), plus
    50g/2oz/½ cup for dusting
50g/2oz/½ cup plain (all-purpose) flour
30ml/2 tbsp ghee or unsalted (sweet)
    butter, plus 10ml/2 tsp, melted
water, to mix
salt

1 Sift the flours and salt into a bowl.
Make a well in the centre and add
10ml/2 tsp of unmelted ghee and fold
into the flour to make a crumbly texture.
Gradually add water to make a soft,
pliable dough. Knead until smooth.
Cover and leave to rest for 30 minutes.

2 Divide the dough into 12–15 equal
portions and keep covered. Take one
portion at a time and roll out on a
lightly floured surface to about 10cm/4in
in diameter. Brush the dough with a little
of the melted ghee or sweet butter and
sprinkle with chapati flour.

3 With a sharp knife, make a straight
cut from the centre to the edge of the
dough, then lift a cut edge and roll
the dough into a cone shape. Lift it and
flatten it again into a ball. Roll the dough
again on a lightly floured surface until it
is 18cm/7in wide.

4 Heat a griddle and cook one paratha
at a time, placing a little of the remaining
ghee along the edges. Cook on each side
until golden brown. Serve hot.

COOK'S TIP

If you cannot find chapati flour, known
as atta, substitute an equal quantity of
wholemeal flour and plain flour.

MISSI ROTIS

These delicious unleavened breads are a speciality from Punjab in India. Gram flour, known as besan, is made from chickpeas and is combined here with the more traditional wheat flour. In Punjab, missi rotis are very popular with a glass of lassi, a refreshing yogurt drink.

MAKES 4

115g/4oz/1 cup gram flour (besan)
115g/4oz/1 cup wholemeal (whole-wheat)
   flour
1 fresh green chilli, seeded and chopped
½ onion, finely chopped
15ml/1 tbsp chopped fresh coriander
   (cilantro)
2.5ml/½ tsp ground turmeric
2.5ml/½ tsp salt
15ml/1 tbsp vegetable oil or melted butter
120–150ml/4–5fl oz/½–⅔ cup lukewarm
   water
30–45ml/2–3 tbsp melted unsalted (sweet)
   butter or ghee

1 Mix the two types of flour, chilli, onion, coriander, turmeric and salt together in a large bowl. Stir in the 15ml/1 tbsp oil or melted butter.

2 Mix in sufficient water to make a pliable soft dough. Turn out the dough on to a lightly floured surface and knead until smooth.

3 Place in a lightly oiled bowl, cover with lightly oiled clear film (plastic wrap) and leave to rest for 30 minutes.

4 Turn the dough out on to a lightly floured surface. Divide into four equal pieces and shape into balls in the palms of your hands. Roll out each ball into a thick round about 15–18cm/6–7in in diameter.

5 Heat a griddle or heavy frying pan over a medium heat for a few minutes until hot.

6 Brush both sides of one roti with some melted butter or ghee. Add it to the griddle or frying pan and cook for about 2 minutes, turning after 1 minute. Brush the cooked roti lightly with melted butter or ghee again, slide it on to a plate and keep warm in a low oven while cooking the remaining rotis in the same way. Serve the rotis warm.

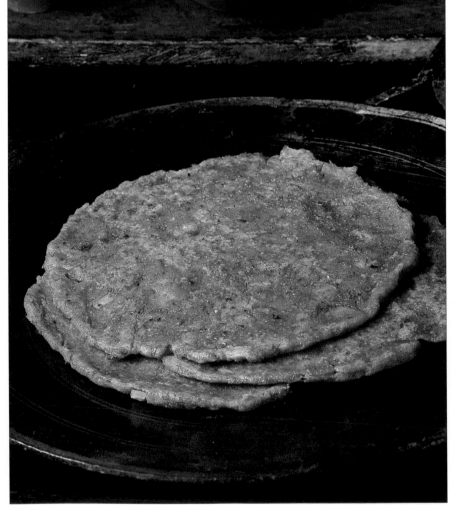

TANDOORI ROTIS

Roti *means bread and is the most common food eaten in central and northern India. For generations, roti has been made with just wholemeal flour, salt and water, although the art of making rotis is generally more refined these days. Tandoori roti is traditionally baked in a tandoor, or clay oven, but it can also be made successfully in an electric or gas oven at the highest setting.*

MAKES 6

350g/12oz/3 cups chapati flour or ground
    wholemeal (whole-wheat) flour
5ml/1 tsp salt
250ml/8fl oz/1 cup water
30–45ml/2–3 tbsp melted ghee or unsalted
    (sweet) butter, for brushing

1 Sift the flour and salt into a large mixing bowl. Add the water and mix to a soft, pliable dough.

2 Knead on a lightly floured surface for 3–4 minutes until smooth. Place the dough in a lightly oiled bowl, cover with lightly oiled clear film (plastic wrap) and leave to rest for 1 hour.

3 Turn out the dough on to a lightly floured surface. Divide the dough into six pieces and shape each into a ball. Press out into a larger round with the palm of your hand, cover with lightly oiled clear film and leave to rest for about 10 minutes.

4 Meanwhile, preheat the oven to 230°C/450°F/Gas 8. Place three baking sheets in the oven to heat. Roll the rotis into 15cm/6in rounds, place two on each baking sheet and bake for 8–10 minutes. Brush with melted ghee or butter and serve warm.

POORIS

These delicious little deep-fried breads, shaped into discs, make it temptingly easy to overindulge. In most areas, they are made of wholemeal flour, but in the east and north-east of India, they are made from plain refined flour, and are known as loochis.

MAKES 12

115g/4oz/1 cup unbleached plain
   (all-purpose) flour
115g/4oz/1 cup wholemeal (whole-wheat)
   flour
2.5ml/½ tsp salt
2.5ml/½ tsp chilli powder
30ml/2 tbsp vegetable oil
100–120ml/3½–4fl oz/scant ⅓–½ cup
   water
oil, for frying

VARIATION
For spinach-flavoured pooris, thaw 50g/2oz frozen spinach, drain, and add to the dough with a little grated fresh root ginger and 2.5ml/½ tsp ground cumin.

1 Sift the flours, salt and chilli powder, if using, into a large mixing bowl. Add the vegetable oil then add sufficient water to mix to a dough. Turn out on to a lightly floured surface and knead for 8–10 minutes until smooth.

2 Place in an oiled bowl and cover with oiled clear film (plastic wrap). Leave for 30 minutes.

3 Turn out on to the floured surface. Divide the dough into 12 equal pieces. Keeping the rest of the dough covered, roll one piece into a 13cm/5in round. Repeat with the remaining dough. Stack the pooris, layered between clear film, to keep them moist.

4 Pour the oil for frying to a depth of 2.5cm/1in in a deep frying pan and heat it to 180°C/350°F. Using a metal fish slice (spatula), lift one poori and gently slide it into the oil; it will sink but will then return to the surface and begin to sizzle. Gently press the poori into the oil. It will puff up. Turn the poori over after a few seconds and allow it to cook for a further 20–30 seconds.

5 Remove the poori from the pan and pat dry with kitchen paper. Place the cooked poori on a large baking tray, in a single layer, and keep warm in a low oven while you cook the remaining pooris. Serve warm.

BHATURAS

These leavened and deep-fried breads are from Punjab, where the local people enjoy them with a bowl of spicy chickpea curry. The combination has become a classic over the years and is known as choley bhature. *Bhaturas must be eaten hot and cannot be reheated.*

MAKES 10 BHATURAS

15g/½oz fresh yeast
5ml/1 tsp granulated sugar
120ml/4fl oz/½ cup lukewarm water
200g/7oz/1¾ cups plain (all-purpose) flour
50g/2oz/½ cup semolina
2.5ml/½ tsp salt
15g/½oz/1 tbsp ghee or butter
30ml/2 tbsp natural (plain) yogurt
oil, for frying

COOK'S TIP

Ghee is availabe from Indian stores and some supermarkets. However, it is easy to make at home. Melt unsalted (sweet) butter over a low heat. Simmer very gently until the residue becomes light golden, then leave to cool. Strain through muslin (cheesecloth) before using.

1 Mix the yeast with the sugar and water in a jug (pitcher). Sift the flour into a large bowl and stir in the semolina and salt. Rub in the butter or ghee.

2 Add the yeast mixture and yogurt and mix to a dough. Turn out on to a lightly floured surface and knead for 10 minutes until smooth and elastic.

3 Place the dough in an oiled bowl, cover with oiled clear film (plastic wrap) and leave to rise, in a warm place, for about 1 hour, or until doubled in size.

4 Turn out on to a lightly floured surface and knock back (punch down). Divide into ten equal pieces and shape each into a ball. Flatten into discs with the palm of your hand. Roll out on a lightly floured surface into 13cm/5in rounds.

5 Heat oil to a depth of 1cm/½in in a deep frying pan and slide one bhatura into the oil. Fry for about 1 minute, turning over after 30 seconds, then drain well on kitchen paper. Keep each bhatura warm in a low oven while frying the remaining bhaturas. Serve immediately, while hot.

CHUTNEYS, PICKLES AND SALADS

Indians believe that eating sour foods with a meal is good for the health,
and they have created a huge range of tart, tangy chutneys and pickles,
refreshing yogurt-based raitas, and raw vegetable salads, which all taste
good with hot, spicy dishes.

MANGO, CORIANDER and TOMATO CHUTNEYS

*Chutneys are always vegetarian, but ingredients vary between regions. Mango and tomato
chutneys are made all over India, while herb chutneys are eaten in the north and west.*

MANGO CHUTNEY

MAKES 450G/1LB/2 CUPS

3 firm green mangoes, cut into chunks
150ml/¼ pint/⅔ cup cider vinegar
130g/4½oz/⅔ cup light muscovado
   (brown) sugar
1 small fresh red chilli, split
2.5cm/1in piece resh root ginger, grated
1 garlic clove, crushed
5 cardamom pods, bruised
2.5ml/½ tsp coriander seeds, crushed
1 bay leaf
2.5ml/½ tsp salt

1 Put the mango chunks into a pan, add
the cider vinegar and cover. Cook over
a low heat for 10 minutes, then stir in
the remaining ingredients. Bring to the
boil slowly, stirring.

2 Lower the heat and simmer gently for
30 minutes, until the mixture is syrupy.
Leave to cool, then ladle into a hot
sterilized jar and cover. Leave to rest for
1 week before serving.

CORIANDER CHUTNEY

MAKES 400G/14OZ/1¾ CUPS

30ml/2 tbsp vegetable oil
1 dried red chilli
1.5ml/¼ tsp each cumin, fennel and
   onion seeds
1.5ml/¼ tsp asafoetida
4 curry leaves
115g/4oz desiccated (dry, unsweetened,
   shredded) coconut
10ml/2 tsp granulated sugar
3 fresh green chillies, chopped
175–225g/6–8oz coriander (cilantro) leaves
60ml/4 tbsp mint sauce
juice of 3 lemons
salt

1 Heat the oil and fry the next eight
ingredients until the coconut turns
golden. Season and allow to cool.

2 Use a mortar and pestle to grind the
spice mixture with the chillies, coriander
and mint sauce. Stir in the lemon juice.
Transfer to a sterilized jar, cover and chill.

TOMATO CHUTNEY

MAKES 450–500G/16–18OZ/2–2¼ CUPS

90ml/6 tbsp vegetable oil
5cm/2in piece cinnamon stick
4 cloves
5ml/1 tsp freshly roasted cumin seeds
5ml/1 tsp nigella seeds
4 bay leaves
5ml/1 tsp mustard seeds, crushed
4 cloves garlic, crushed
5cm/2in piece fresh root ginger, grated
5ml/1 tsp chilli powder
5ml/1 tsp ground turmeric
60ml/4 tbsp brown sugar
800g/¾lb canned, chopped tomatoes,
   drained, juices reserved

1 Heat the oil, then fry the first six
spices. Add the garlic and fry until golden.

2 Add the remaining spices, sugar and
reserved tomato juices. Simmer until
reduced, then add the tomatoes and
cook for 15–20 minutes. Leave to cool,
then ladle into a sterilized jar and cover.

MINT and COCONUT, APRICOT and TOMATO and FRESH CHILLI CHUTNEYS

Chutneys can be made by grinding fresh ingredients together, or by slow-cooking.

MINT AND COCONUT CHUTNEY

MAKES ABOUT 350ML/12FL OZ/1½ CUPS

50g/2oz fresh mint leaves
90ml/6 tbsp desiccated (dry, unsweetened, shredded) coconut
15ml/1 tbsp sesame seeds
1.5ml/¼ tsp salt
175ml/6fl oz/¾ cup natural (plain) yogurt

1 Finely chop the fresh mint leaves, using a sharp kitchen knife.

2 Put all the ingredients into a food processor or blender and process until smooth. Transfer to a sterilized jar, cover and chill until needed.

COOK'S TIP
This chutney can be stored in the refrigerator for up to 5 days.

APRICOT CHUTNEY

MAKES ABOUT 450G/1LB/2 CUPS

450g/1lb/2 cups dried apricots, finely diced
5ml/1 tsp garam masala
275g/10oz/1¼ cups soft light brown sugar
450ml/¾ pint/scant 2 cups malt vinegar
5ml/1 tsp grated fresh root ginger
5ml/1 tsp salt
75g/3oz/½ cup sultanas (golden raisins)
450ml/¾ pint/scant 2 cups water

1 Put all the ingredients together into a pan and stir well to mix. Bring to the boil, then simmer for 30–35 minutes, stirring occasionally.

2 When the chutney becomes syrupy, remove from the heat. Leave to cool, then ladle into a hot sterilized jar and cover. Chill after opening.

TOMATO AND FRESH CHILLI CHUTNEY

MAKES ABOUT 475ML/16FL OZ/2 CUPS

1 red (bell) pepper
4 tomatoes, chopped
2 fresh green chillies, chopped
1 garlic clove, crushed
1.5ml/¼ tsp salt
2.5ml/½ tsp granulated sugar
5ml/1 tsp chilli powder
45ml/3 tbsp tomato purée (paste)
15ml/1 tbsp chopped fresh coriander (cilantro)

1 Halve the red pepper and remove the core and seeds. Roughly chop the red pepper halves.

2 Process all the ingredients with 30ml/ 2 tbsp water in a food processor until smooth. Transfer to a sterilized jar, cover and chill until needed.

BOMBAY DUCK PICKLE

Boil is the name of a fish that is found off the west coast of India during the monsoon season. It is salted and dried in the sun and is characterized by a strong smell and distinctive piquancy. How this fish acquired the name Bombay duck in the Western world is still unknown. Bombay duck can be served hot or cold, and is usually eaten with Indian breads as an accompaniment to vegetable dishes.

SERVES 4–6

6–8 pieces boil (Bombay duck), soaked
   in water for 5 minutes
60ml/4 tbsp vegetable oil
2 fresh red chillies, chopped
15ml/1 tbsp granulated sugar
450g/1lb cherry tomatoes, halved
115g/4oz deep-fried onions
red onion rings, to garnish (optional)

COOK'S TIP

As an alternative to boil, try skinned mackeral fillets, without frying them. You will need only 30ml/2 tbsp vegetable oil to make the sauce.

1 Pat the fish dry with kitchen paper. Heat the oil in a frying pan and fry the fish pieces for about 30–45 seconds on both sides until crisp. Be careful not to burn them as they will taste bitter. Drain well. When cool, break into small pieces.

2 Cook the remaining ingredients until the tomatoes become pulpy and the onions are blended into a sauce. Fold in the Bombay duck and mix well. Leave to cool, then garnish and serve, or ladle into a hot sterilized jar and cover.

HOT LIME PICKLE and GREEN CHILLI PICKLE

*Spicy pickles are a perennial favourite with all types of curry. Leaving the pickles to rest
for a week after preparation will greatly enhance the flavours.*

HOT LIME PICKLE

MAKES 450G/1LB/2 CUPS

25 limes, cut into wedges
225g/8oz/1 cup salt
50g/2oz/¼ cup fenugreek powder
50g/2oz/¼ cup mustard powder
150g/5oz/¾ cup chilli powder
15ml/1 tbsp ground turmeric
600ml/1 pint/2½ cups mustard oil
5ml/1 tsp asafoetida
25g/1oz yellow mustard seeds, crushed

1 Place the limes in a large sterilized jar
or glass bowl. Add the salt and toss with
the limes. Cover and leave in a warm
place for 1–2 weeks, until they become
soft and dull brown in colour.

2 Mix the fenugreek, mustard powder,
chilli powder and turmeric and add to
the limes. Cover and leave to rest in
a warm place for a further 2–3 days.

3 Heat the oil and fry the asafoetida
and mustard seeds. When the oil
reaches smoking point, pour it over the
limes. Mix well. Cover and leave in a
warm place for 1 week before serving.

GREEN CHILLI PICKLE

MAKES 450–550G/1–1¼LB/2–2½ CUPS

50g/2oz/¼ cup mustard seeds,
    crushed
50g/2oz/¼ cup freshly ground
    cumin seeds
25ml/1½ tbsp ground turmeric
50g/2oz/¼ cup crushed garlic
150ml/¼ pint/⅔ cup white vinegar
75g/3oz/scant ½ cup granulated sugar
10ml/2 tsp salt
150ml/¼ pint/⅔ cup mustard oil
20 small garlic cloves
450g/1lb small fresh green
    chillies, halved

1 Mix the mustard seeds, cumin,
turmeric, crushed garlic, vinegar, sugar
and salt in a sterilized jar or glass bowl.
Cover and allow to rest for 24 hours.
This enables the spices to infuse
(steep) and the sugar and salt to melt.

2 Heat the mustard oil and gently fry
the spice mixture for about 5 minutes.
(Keep a window open while cooking
with mustard oil as it is pungent and the
smoke may irritate the eyes.) Add the
whole garlic cloves and fry for a further
5 minutes.

3 Add the halved fresh chillies and cook
gently until tender but still green in
colour. This will take about 30 minutes
on a low heat. Cool thoroughly.

4 Pour into the sterilized jar, ensuring
that the oil is evenly distributed if you
are using more than one bottle. Leave
to rest for 1 week before serving.

SPICED YOGURT and CUCUMBER RAITA

These slightly sour, yogurt-based accompaniments have a cooling effect on the palate when eaten with spicy foods, and they help to balance the flavours of an Indian meal.

SPICED YOGURT

MAKES 450ML/¾ PINT/SCANT 2 CUPS

450ml/¾ pint/scant 2 cups natural (plain)
   yogurt
2.5ml/½ tsp freshly ground fennel seeds
2.5ml/½ tsp granulated sugar
60ml/4 tbsp vegetable oil
I dried red chilli
1.5ml/¼ tsp mustard seeds
1.5ml/¼ tsp cumin seeds
4–6 curry leaves
a pinch each of asafoetida and
   ground turmeric
salt

I Mix together the yogurt, fennel and sugar, and add salt to taste. Chill.

2 Heat the oil and fry the remaining ingredients. When the chilli turns dark, pour the oil and spices over the yogurt and mix. Cover and chill before serving.

CUCUMBER RAITA

MAKES ABOUT 600ML/I PINT/2½ CUPS

½ cucumber
I fresh green chilli, seeded and chopped
300ml/½ pint/1¼ cups natural (plain)
   yogurt
1.5ml/¼ tsp salt
1.5ml/¼ tsp ground cumin

I Dice the cucumber finely and place in a large mixing bowl. Add the chilli.

2 Beat the natural yogurt with a fork until smooth, then stir into the cucumber and chilli mixture.

3 Stir in the salt and cumin. Cover the bowl with clear film (plastic wrap) and chill before serving.

VARIATION
Instead of cucumber, use two skinned, seeded and chopped tomatoes and 15ml/ I tbsp chopped fresh coriander (cilantro).

FRUIT RAITA and TOMATO and ONION SALAD

*Refreshing yogurt raitas can be made with almost any fruit. Raw vegetable salads, known
as cachumbers, are another classic way of adding a tangy touch to a meal.*

FRUIT RAITA

SERVES 4

350ml/12fl oz/1½ cups natural
(plain) yogurt
75g/3oz seedless grapes, washed and dried
50g/2oz shelled walnuts
2 firm bananas, sliced
5ml/1 tsp granulated sugar
5ml/1 tsp freshly ground cumin seeds
salt
1.5ml/¼ tsp freshly roasted cumin seeds,
chilli powder, to garnish

1 Put the yogurt, grapes and walnuts in
a bowl. Fold in the bananas.

2 Stir in the sugar, ground cumin and salt.
Chill and sprinkle on the roasted cumin
seeds and chilli powder before serving.

TOMATO AND ONION SALAD

SERVES 4–6

2 limes
2.5ml/½ tsp granulated sugar
a few fresh coriander (cilantro) sprigs,
chopped, plus extra for garnishing
2 onions, finely chopped
4 firm tomatoes, finely chopped
½ cucumber, finely chopped
1 fresh green chilli, finely chopped
salt and ground black pepper
a few fresh mint sprigs, to garnish

1 Extract the juice of the limes into
a small bowl. Add the sugar, salt and
pepper and allow to rest until the sugar
and salt have competely dissolved. Mix
together well.

2 Add the remaining ingredients and
mix well. Chill, and garnish with fresh
coriander and mint sprigs before serving.

VARIATION
For Banana and Coconut Raita, slice
2 bananas and fold into 350ml/12fl oz/
1½ cups natural yogurt. Stir in 30ml/2 tbsp
desiccated coconut and add a pinch of chilli
powder, and salt and lemon juice to taste.

INDEX